Queen of Kingston

BOOK 5 OF THE QUEENS OF THE CASTLE SERIES

J.L. CAMPBELL &
PAT G'ORGE-WALKER

This is a work of fiction. Names, characters, places, and incidents are products of the author's imagination or are used fictitiously and are not to be construed as real. Any resemblance to actual events, locales, organizations, or persons, living or dead, is entirely coincidental.

Queen of Kingston by J. L. Campbell & Pat G'Orge Walker Copyright ©2021
Ebook ISBN - 978-976-8307-18-7
Trade Paperback ISBN 978-976-8307-17-0

Cover Designed by: J.L Woodson: www.woodsoncreativestudio.com
Interior Designed by: Lissa Woodson: www.naleighnakai.com
Editor: Lissa Woodson: www.naleighnakai.com
Queen of Kingston 5

Queen of Kingston

BOOK 5 OF THE QUEENS OF THE CASTLE SERIES

J.L. CAMPBELL &
PAT G'ORGE-WALKER

ACKNOWLEDGEMENT

Thanks to Naleighna Kai for conceptualizing and including us in the world of the Kings, Knights & Queens of the Castle. Your editing pen keeps us striving to write better stories.

No book is complete without beta readers. Many thanks to D.J. Mitchell, Marie McKenzie, and Christine Pauls for their laser-sharp focus and the investment of their time and energy.

Karen D. Bradley and Naleighna Kai were gracious enough to let us use their characters and gizmos in the world of the Queens.

J.L. Woodson, keep on shining through the outstanding artistry you bring to each cover.

Without readers, writers have no platform. Many thanks to the faithful readers who have followed our stories through the years. We love and appreciate you!

The Kings of the Castle Ambassadors and readers in the Naleighna Kai Literary Café have also been a source of encouragement and support.

Thank you!

Chapter 1

Don't look at me like that, I told you this would happen.

Samantha stared at Kingston over her parents' dining table, wishing the evening was over. Despite the pleasant surroundings—a dining room filled with expensive furnishings and paintings—the air simmered with nasty undercurrents.

Earlier, she warned him what Mom and Papa's reaction would be to their relationship, but he insisted on coming. "What sense does it make to visit Jamaica and not meet your family?" he'd asked.

She hadn't answered because she understood them, but wasn't ready to deal with their hang-ups and old-fashioned thinking. Kingston's deep-bronze complexion, spiky hair, and almond-shaped eyes would send their stress level into the stratosphere.

Her father, Elias, a stocky, balding man with pale skin, laid his cutlery down and wiped his lips with a napkin. "So, Kingston, do you still have family on the island?"

"My grandmother lives in Clarendon, but my immediate family is in New York." His gaze met hers. "That's where I met Sam."

Sharon DaCosta straightened in her chair and swallowed the Chinese roast chicken as if it had suddenly developed a bitter taste. "*Samantha* insisted on going to university there, against our wishes."

Speaking in a pointed way, Papa glanced around the table. "Aside from getting an education, our daughter came home with radical ideas."

Which includes a relationship with a half-breed Black man.

Nobody said the words, but Sharon DaCosta turned up her nose while pushing aside several blonde strands that escaped from beneath her purple headband decorated with faux pearls. "At least, she kept her gorgeous hair. We were afraid she might've changed it to fit in with her liberal thinking."

She sneered as if Kingston was a bit of refuse one of their spoiled dogs had brought in from the garden.

Michele, her younger sister by two years, rubbed Sam's foot under the table and offered a smile, a gesture of solidarity. She still lived at home, despite being thirty. Their three-story house in Red Hills was the perfect creative environment for her fashion studio, and with her parents' blessing, she commandeered the top floor of the house and came and went as it suited her.

"Sam," Michele said, nodding in their mother's direction, "remember di time when you and Mom wanted to get dem brownish highlights?"

Her sister had never been constrained by societal norms and was classified by the people who knew her as "down to earth," or "roots" in Jamaican terms. Perhaps that was why their father had never pressured her. She was the baby of the family and her colorful personality had revealed itself in her toddler years when she refused to wear disposable diapers and would rip them off as often as their helper caught her and sealed her inside a new one. Now, she had slipped into Patois and added that comment to provoke their father. Sam hoped she didn't have more zingers in her arsenal.

"Enough," Elias' eyes bulged as he seethed. Displeasure turned his complexion corpse-gray. Glancing towards Kingston, he declared. "I said it before and I'll say it again. Your hair is part of your European heritage." Elias took a deep breath as if to allow his meaning to sink in.

"Through the centuries, on your mother's side as well as mine, we've kept certain things pure. And pure, they will stay. There will be no brown highlights in your hair or anyplace else."

"So, Papa, does dat still apply to our friends, near and wide?" A smirk appeared on Michele's face and she giggled behind the napkin.

"I believe people should stick to their own kind."

Sam wished Michele wouldn't provoke him. Aside from the subject matter, the use of Patois grated on their father's nerves and the more irritable he became, the more foolishness spewed from his mouth. Not that Michele cared. They had learned Patois at an early age from the household employees and moved fluently between the local language and the Queen's English. When they were children, Papa forbade them to speak broken English, which guaranteed that Michele goaded him by using it when it suited her.

"I'm as Jamaican as anyone else on this island and will not deny that part of my heritage because you're intolerant," she'd told him years ago, to his horror.

Since that time, his attitude and opinion hadn't changed.

Only God knew what Kingston thought of Elias' petulant, shallow declaration. When Sam peeked at Kingston, his bland expression seemed to match Michele's. Perhaps they were kindred spirits. He was certainly taking this display of bad behavior better than Sam, but her perception changed when their eyes met and she felt the heat in his gaze.

Michele's eyes sparkled, and Sam knew she wasn't finished.

With a curious expression in place, she asked, "Do you think Papa meant anything specific? Perhaps, being blonde sets you apart from other affluent people of color in our society." She winked and lowered her head, a habit that surfaced whenever she threw a verbal brick before hiding her hands.

"Doesn't matter to me," Sam replied, despite the rabid way she stabbed the food on her plate. The unpleasant conversation had killed her appetite.

Years ago, Sam grew tired of the weight of her parents' expectations and put as much distance as possible between herself and the family. Even now, her father resented the fact that she got along better with his only brother, Edward, or Ted, as she called him. He had facilitated Sam's flight to freedom and Elias had never forgiven him for it.

"Have you heard from Edward recently?" he asked.

Sam stopped frowning and dropped the fork on her plate with a clang. "As a matter of fact, he spoke with me yesterday."

The mention of his name brought back her anxiety. Sam was working on several stories for the newspaper—one about a brilliant teenager and another about The Castle, a humanitarian organization based in Chicago. Ted was a member of The Castle, but in her research, Sam had stumbled across his name on a list that jarred her. If she could believe it, her uncle had been part of something that might be considered nefarious. But she wouldn't condemn him without speaking to him. He was the first person on her list to contact when she was back in the States.

Rose, their helper, came in to clear the table for dessert. Her cheerful smile and twinkling eyes reminded Sam of the many hours spent with her around the house during her childhood. Whenever she was feeling down, Rose reminded her of the many advantages and blessings she had that other people didn't. She winked at Rose, who stifled a smile.

"Given what you went through in high school, I'm not sure how or why you two connected in this way."

The shock that flickered over Rose's face and dimmed her eyes confirmed that Sharon had abandoned good manners and civility. Not to mention the sudden change in the direction of their conversation, something she reserved for whenever Ted's name was mentioned.

Sam looked directly at her mother. "I'm not one to stay stuck in the past, so …"

"And I'm not as diplomatic as your mother." Papa pushed his plate aside and leaned back in his oversized chair, one reserved for his girth and status as head of the family.

With an air of authority, he studied each person at the table while his fingers carved a path through a sparse patch of dark hair. He did it when displeased, and now wagged his finger at Samantha.

"The last time you came home, you brought visitors, claiming they were going to be Queens. Delusional. If you don't deal with your past, it will ruin more than your future." With disdain etched on his features, he glanced at Kingston. "I would add that unlearned lessons will taint your present, as well."

The off-hand mention of Cassandra Toussaint, Queen of Curaçao, and Milan Germaine, Queen of Wilmette, roused her annoyance. These were her sister-friends he was disparaging. Members of The Castle with skills and talents her father couldn't even begin to imagine. On top of that, they had a heart for service—unlike her family. Sam's glare found its mark and she didn't hide her anger. Her slender fingers formed a steeple on which she rested her chin.

"Speaking of the past, present, and future," Sam's voice rose with each word. "Have you ever asked Mom if *you* were her *first* choice?"

Elias sprang forward and his weight tilted the chair. "What do you mean?"

His face reddened and a bluish halo appeared around his jowls as though he were about to have a heart attack, or was in the middle of one.

"Has the devil descended in my home?" he snarled as he looked at his wife, then pointed at Samantha. "Sharon, what is she talking about? What does she mean by asking me such a question?"

"The same thing I always mean when posing issues, and you deflect." Sam's voice intensified to match the fervor of her father's. "This time, leave Mom out of this. She may have started it, but this conversation is between me and you, Papa."

"In my home, I decide who a conversation is between. Always has been and always will be." His dictatorial words tore through the air and hung in the bitter silence.

Kingston dropped the linen napkin on the table. "Sir, that is totally uncalled for."

Her father's skin turned a blotchy red. "You, of all people, don't get to tell me what is appropriate in my home."

Pushing back from the table, Kingston rose. "Since it's *me of all people*, and I've figured out this is the way it's going to be, we'll bid you good evening."

Sam and her mother stood at the same time.

"Where are you going?" Sharon asked. Her words said one thing, but a gloss crept across her eyes, turning her question into a plea.

"We're leaving the island tomorrow, anyway. So, it's just as well that I get out of this house tonight."

"I've put up with a lot from you over the years and supported you, even when I didn't believe in what you were doing." Papa tipped his head back to meet Sam's gaze. "But this is different. If you leave here like this, don't come back."

His words had the effect of a throat punch, and tears of frustration seared her eyes. The rash statement that came to her lips couldn't make their way past the tightness in her throat.

Sharon stared at Elias. Her mouth opened and closed several times.

The color drained from Michele's face, leaving her looking like a ghost. The cloud of black hair contrasted with her pasty skin.

Sam turned a desperate gaze on Kingston, whose onyx-colored eyes were closed to slits. She wanted out.

He understood her non-verbal message immediately and button-holed her father with a searing look that matched Elias' glare—checkmate. Kingston saved her from saying anything she'd regret by gently leading her from the room.

When they stood in the foyer, close to the front door, Kingston cupped her face and whispered, "I'm so sorry. Can you manage?"

Her mother's pair of tan Shih Tzu rushed toward them and swirled around their ankles as if they understood Sam's need for comfort.

She stroked Kingston's cheek and nudged the dogs out of the way. "I'll go upstairs and get my things, then come right down."

His encouraging smile gave Sam the boost she needed to move her heavy feet.

Kingston swiped the tear from the corner of her eye with his thumb and kissed her forehead. "I'll be waiting."

Chapter 2

"The next time my daughter's idiot husband makes you angry, please think before you act."

"Yes, Grandma Esmie." Sam's tone was penitent. Only her grandmother could get that reaction from her.

"That doesn't mean I'm taking their side," she continued. "I'm just upset because you and Kingston didn't come and see me again before flying out."

"I'm sorry. That wasn't intentional." Sam lowered the screen of her laptop and walked around the luxurious suite. "Tell me something though, how come you think so differently from them and you're older."

A few seconds went by before her grandmother said, "I was lucky that when my marriage was arranged, my father understood that I didn't like the man they chose for me. He was a widower and much older than I was. Times were different, but I guess the situation worked out for me because the man I truly loved was also Lebanese and that was acceptable to the family."

"So what happened with Mom?" Sam perched on the sofa and scanned the living room, smiling softly when her gaze landed on the basket of fruits and specialty chocolate Kingston had sent a day after they arrived in Chicago.

They flew from Jamaica to New York's Kennedy International Airport and did something different. Rather than going to their respective homes, they stayed at a hotel in Manhattan. After that chaotic scene at her parents' home, having that intimate time with Kingston in an unfamiliar space was what she wanted. It was also what she needed. The questions she had for Ted could wait until after she repaired the damage her family had done to their relationship. When she had no one else, Kingston stood at her side.

Among their plans was an evening in a Jazz Club on Forty-second Street and visiting some of their old haunts. But once they stepped into the shower together, plans for the Jazz Club faded.

Although Kingston's singing was out of tune and would've caused a cat to scratch out his eyeballs, his love-making with Sam was always in the right key. For the next several hours, he had her singing a different tune in each section of the three room-suite.

Sam crooned "A Whole New World" all the way to "You Make Me Feel Brand New." Just before they'd collapsed from everything they hadn't tried before, Kingston belted, "I Just Can't Wait to Be King."

Two days later, they flew to Chicago based on her need to speak with her uncle. She had continued working on her story and was even more disturbed than she'd been the previous week. Ted had given her permission to occupy one of the bedrooms in his suite at The Castle, and she expected him to return from a business trip this afternoon. Kingston was staying at a friend's apartment nearby.

Sam's mind returned to the conversation when her grandmother said, "Your mother has always been spineless. I only found out after she was engaged to *him* that she had someone else in her life." Her grandmother sighed. "Elias is the strong one in that marriage. Whatever he tells her, Sharon is going to do, no matter how she feels about it. Including trying to run your life and decide who you marry."

Her parents thought it was perfectly all right to make their money off the local population with their movie theater and superstores, but someone of Kingston's color was off-limits.

"It really doesn't matter," she said. "Thank goodness, I don't depend on them for money, so they can take their opinion and stuff it—"

"Careful, Samantha, despite how unenlightened they are, some respect is due."

"Whatever you say, Grandma."

The older woman chuckled, and Samatha pictured the skin around her eyes creasing as she absorbed Sam's snarky response. Grandma Esmie still lived on her own and took care of herself at the ripe old age of eighty-five. The only concession she made to dependency was a housekeeper, who came in twice each week, and the cameras she allowed Sam's father to install inside and outside of her home.

"Give it time, they'll come around," Grandma Esmie said, "Kingston looks like a sensible man. If he's the one, you'll both be all right with each other. I know you have to work, but don't wait too long to call me."

"I won't." Samantha made kissing sounds, then went back to the writing desk to one side of the lounge. She tucked one corner of her lip into her mouth. She had met Kingston at the university, but they remained on the periphery of each other's lives. Four years previously, they crossed paths at the newspaper, where he was a political reporter. At the time, she'd been dabbling in the society pages.

Her qualification in the social sciences made her long for more than tracking social functions and mixing with the glam crowd. When she had the chance to work on human interest stories, she grabbed the opportunity with both hands. One of her articles had a political angle and that's how she re-connected with Kingston, who was also a civil rights lawyer.

He'd filled out and was brawny, with probing, dark eyes that seemed to pierce the depths of her soul. The low stubble on his jaw made her fingers itch to touch his skin.

Was he the one? After these many months she still didn't know, but suspected her reluctance to dive deeper into her emotions came from family expectations. Kingston didn't look like any of her relatives, at least none that were acknowledged. Even as she grew into their relationship, Sam knew her family would be one of their biggest hurdles. The other was Kingston's attitude toward how she did her job. She, also, had the same issue with him.

The door to the suite opened and her uncle walked into the room. Ted was the opposite of his older brother. He was tall and lanky and though his sandy blond hair was thinning, he still turned heads. His olive skin was darker than Elias', but the thin nose with a fleshy tip under thick eyebrows and intense eyes provided a striking family resemblance.

His deep-hazel gaze lit with affection when she met him halfway across the room.

"How's my favorite niece," he asked, as they hugged.

"Fair to fine," she answered. "You know how it is."

"How's the family," he asked, shrugging out of his jacket. He beckoned to the valet, who arrived with his small suitcase.

The uniformed man rolled it into the room and departed when Ted told him it was fine to leave it by the door.

Ted disappeared for a moment, then returned with a bottle of spring water. "So, what brings you here?" he asked, sitting across from her in a Queen Anne wingback chair.

She settled on one of the sofas and curled her legs. "Remember I told you I was doing some research for an article?"

He sipped from the bottle, then nodded. "That sounds like regular stuff."

"Yes, but I came across your name in some documents connected to MiVaxx Incorporated and thought I'd get some clarity from you."

Her imagination might have been working overtime, but Sam thought her uncle stiffened before he grinned and set the bottle on the table next to him. "You're always working on a story. What company did you name just now? I'm on the board of several so forgive me if …" He shrugged and didn't continue.

She enunciated the name slowly, concerned that something was amiss. Why was he acting as if the organization was strange to him, especially since she knew he'd been appointed to the board less than a year ago?

Instead of blurting an accusation, Sam looked away to cover her exasperation. He was lying, and the weight of the unnecessary deceit took her breath away.

"That's fine, *Uncle* Ted, but I know your brain still works." Sam winked. "This is me. Sam. Your *favorite niece*. Spill the tea."

"Spill the tea?" Ted gave a shy grin as he patted the thinning hairs on his head. "Even I, an old man, must give homage to the use of the well-known Internet phrase for telling secrets and revealing the hidden truths."

"Stop dodging. Come on and spill it," Sam wheedled, leaning toward him. "You know that I know that *you* know what I meant the first time."

Sam's usual sing-song way of prodding her uncle to relax and chat failed.

"I promise I will look it up, and if this company …" Ted rubbed his chin before raising his head. "What was the company name?" He chuckled, and the hand supporting his chin shook slightly. "Your uncle is getting older. My memory is shorter."

Ted was only sixty, so hiding behind age was another clue something was wrong. Despite the impression he gave of being relaxed, Ted couldn't stop fidgeting. He shouldn't be this uncomfortable if he didn't know about the underhanded activity the company was engaged in.

"Remember I won't be here long, so I'd like that information before I leave Chicago."

She studied him closely, waiting for what he'd say next.

Chapter 3

Hiding his concern, Kingston watched Sam, who frowned at one of the skyscrapers a few feet away. Her hazel gaze was unfocused, which told him she was staring beyond the artwork.

They stood inside the Chicago Architecture Center, filled with famous and impressive displays of various neighborhoods and buildings with interesting designs.

With one finger, Kingston tipped Sam's chin toward him and looked into her eyes. "What's the matter? You've been a little … no, a lot distracted."

She stared over his shoulder, then said, "I think Ted is in trouble."

He released her chin, frowning. "Why d'you think so? What kind of trouble?"

Sam waited until a small group moved past them and gathered before the next exhibit.

While the docent shared tidbits about the artwork, Sam pulled her bottom lip into her mouth. Then, looking into Kingston's eyes, she said.

"Remember that story about vaccines that were distributed in Kenya?"

Kingston narrowed his eyes until he grasped the memory he'd been searching for. "The ones that caused a range of side effects?"

"Yes, that." She tugged his hand and pulled him aside when another set of visitors approached.

"I believe the company knew exactly what they were doing."

"Whoa. What?"

She nodded and smoothed her hair back with both hands. After a deep breath, Sam continued, "He's been on the board for nearly a year, but I couldn't get him to admit he knew anything was wrong."

"In that situation, you have to understand why he'd keep what he knows close to his chest." Kingston smiled, then added, "You may be his niece, but you're also a newshound."

"You're correct, and I get that."

"He also knows you'll stay true to your story and dig every little detail out of him, whether he wants to give it up or not. You can be very persuasive." Clasping her hand, he asked, "So, what are you going to do?"

Sam gave him a side eye. "Why d'you think I have a plan?"

While tickling her palm, he said, "Because you *always* have one."

She pulled in a deep breath, then said, "You know me too well. I have an idea or two, but I'm not ready to share."

"I hear you." Kingston's arm slipped around Sam's waist as if it had a will of its own. He eased closer, and she tipped her head to kiss the stubble on his jaw.

"I didn't know you were interested in architecture," he said, letting his gaze stray to one of the displays.

"I'm not." She wriggled her eyebrows, then said, "You insisted that we do something to get out, so here we are."

"It was either that or unknot you later, after you turned into a pretzel sitting at that desk."

She cocked one eyebrow. "Weren't you working, too?"

"Yes, love, but you're a workaholic, who doesn't know when to stop," he whispered against her skin, then kissed her forehead.

Looking up at him, Sam smiled. "I could say the same about you when you're pulling your stories together."

"Right, but I don't forget to eat. You do."

They now stood inside the gallery, which was an amazing replica of Chicago's skyscrapers. He could have stayed there all afternoon, but his intention was to keep them moving. Sam's working habits concerned him. She often allowed each project to consume her to the exclusion of everything else. Including him.

As he stroked her arm, two women who stood a few feet away whispered, then looked in his direction and shook their heads. When they eyeballed him again, Kingston raised both eyebrows, waiting for them to be bold enough to say something out of pocket. The pair turned away, but not before giving Sam a thorough once-over and cutting their eyes at him.

Kingston was used to it. Sam and he attracted attention wherever they went. What he didn't like was that people assumed he was betraying his race by having a relationship with her. What others didn't know was that where they came from, financial status mattered more than the color of one's skin. After all, the island's motto was, *Out of many, one people*, and Bob Marley claimed it was all about One Love.

"They don't matter." Sam patted his hand that still rested on her arm.

"How d'you know what I'm thinking?"

"You tensed up like a rattler ready to strike," she teased, tipping her head to one side. "I know that look. I get those same sneers."

"I know you do." Kingston's lips tightened and he clenched his jaw. "And it pisses me off."

The hurt in Sam's eyes muted Kingston's mood, and he turned toward one of the nearby paintings to block out her pain, but only for a second. Anything said or done to bring that look was not on the menu today.

"It's fine, honey."

Kingston nodded and opened his mouth, but Sam took center stage.

The hard edge to her voice should have been a warning. He realized it too late. Sam was going to be Sam and ensure that their unwelcome judges heard what was on her mind. She placed one hand on his shoulder, and with the other, lifted her hair and went for broke.

"You think the kids will mind if mommy and papa stay out just a little longer today?" Sam then glared at the women who now turned to face them. "Especially since we have an *unwelcome* audience, who clearly need entertainment. Don't want to disappoint such judgmental people who have no business of their own, but put their nose so far up everyone else's they can smell their bowels."

The women stood transfixed, mouths agape, then their eyes narrowed at her insolence. The eldest shook her head and they turned away, but not before sending a disparaging look their way.

Sam pulled her lips into a pout and threw them a kiss.

Chuckling at her audacity, Kingston reminded himself that he needed to give Sam his news, sooner rather than later.

They faced each other and she pulled his head down to her and pecked his lips.

"What was that for?" he asked, resting both hands on her shoulders.

"To remind you to stay in the here and now." She patted him on the chest "It's weird how you always know when my mind strays whenever we're in the same space. I feel the same way when yours does, too."

"Really?"

"Uh-huh, but I'll be patient until you tell me what's bugging you."

At times like these, he wanted to hug Sam until she was breathless. They had a connection that was uncommon. But perhaps that was because of their shared experiences. That dinner with her family still stung. He put his thoughts aside and got them moving. "Let's finish the tour, then find something to eat."

They were out of the gallery in another forty-five minutes and went to a restaurant down the street that served Jamaican food. Sam's uncle had let her in on that secret, and she had told Kingston they'd be eating there before they went back to the two-bedroom apartment where he was staying.

The atmosphere was warm and welcoming with soft instrumental reggae in the background. Their waitress was a young woman with gorgeous dark skin and a brilliant smile. She wore a bandana apron over her clothing. The fine plaid was part of Jamaica's national costume and a welcome and familiar sight for Kingston. Sam's grin told him she felt the same way.

"My name is Cassie," the young lady said, while handing them menu cards. "How are you today and may I take your order?"

"It's good to be here." Sam scanned the decor, then focused on their server. "A relative told me about this place."

Her words made the teenager do a double take and cock her head as if she thought Sam was fooling her.

Sam glanced at Kingston, then the waitress, and chuckled. "Yes, you guessed right."

"You're Jamaican?" Cassie asked, raising both eyebrows.

Sam laughed, but it didn't reach her eyes. "I may not look like most of the population, but I sure am."

Nodding, the girl straightened her face. "Right, but I can tell by your accent. So, what are you having?"

"We'll have the special of the day." Kingston handed her the menu card, smiling.

Cassie gave them a mischievous grin as she took Sam's menu. "I'll be right back."

She didn't disappoint, and returned with their appetizer in a few minutes and kept the food coming without any waiting time.

After consuming red peas soup, curried goat, and pumpkin rice with steamed vegetables, Sam quipped. "Ted was right. That meal was fit for a *king*."

He gave her an indulgent look, then shook his head. "That's so corny, I should make you pay for lunch."

Sam laughed because she never lost an opportunity to play on words with his name.

Once he settled the bill, Kingston left Cassie a generous tip, and promised her they would return before leaving Chicago.

"Next time, you better have some grater cake available for me," he said, laughing.

"You like them?" she asked.

"No, love 'em," Kingston said, then explained to Sam that Ted had told him they made the best ones. The concoction of grated coconut, granulated sugar, and vanilla was cooked until sticky, then topped with coconut mixed with a dab of red food coloring.

Still talking about menu items they hadn't eaten in some time, they meandered in silence through several out-of-the-way streets. Their random touches or smiles communicated what spoken words couldn't.

Kingston dropped his arm over Sam's shoulder and kissed her cheek, inhaling the flowery perfume that carried delicate, musky undertones which stirred his libido.

She rubbed her forehead against his neck. "So, are we going back to New York when we leave Chicago?"

Kingston's gaze was quizzical. "Why are you asking that now?"

"You know." They moved past a group of rowdy young men, leaning against a chain fence. Their raucous laughter was accompanied by high-fives, and off-color rapping. She picked up the pace to avoid their childish behavior and silently urged Kingston to do the same by lengthening her steps. "Maybe I should ask what you're working on, because that will give me a better idea of what demon I'll be battling this time."

He drew his arm closer around her. "Come on, Sam. Don't be like that."

"Well, maybe if you just tell me what I want to know ..."

They stopped and he stroked her cheek. "You would choose the middle of the sidewalk to have this kind of discussion."

"You said it," she shot back. "I'm a newshound, so that's part of the landscape."

"I'm not ready to talk about this, but there's a story the company would like me to cover."

She studied him with a mixture of concern and resignation in her gaze. "And you want to go, don't you? Where is it this time?"

He'd never lied to her, so he immediately answered, "China."

Frowning, she said, "Can you tell me what you'll be covering specifically?"

"A story surrounding how Africans have been treated since the outbreak of the Coronavirus."

Sam walked away with both hands in the pockets of her jacket. The distance between them increased with every stride.

When he caught up with her, Kingston gently gripped her arm and kept pace with her.

Avoiding his gaze, she said, "Have you looked at the color of your skin lately?"

His brows dipped into a frown. "What does that have to do with anything?"

"In case you missed it, your eyes may be evidence of your oriental ancestry, but your skin will put you at a disadvantage."

"And when has that ever been different?"

She sighed and kept walking. "We know what to expect in America, but China is half a world away."

"Don't you think I know that?" he countered.

She drew to a halt, her gaze filled with suspicion. "Something tells me you've already decided you're going and that's where I have a problem."

"Let's talk about it later." He rested both hands on her shoulders. "For now, let's concentrate on us. Being together here and now."

A horn blast drowned some of his words and he leaned closer to Sam, who said, "I'm all for that, but please tell me this trip isn't already in motion."

Her close study made him wince and he wasn't surprised when she backed away and continued down the sidewalk ... without him.

Kingston yelled her name, but she didn't break her stride.

Chapter 4

Sam needed Kingston's help, but hated to ask. He always said she was too independent, yet he admired that part of her character. Admiration or not, she hadn't spoken to him since their outing two days ago despite the many calls and texts from him. She could have visited before now, but she'd been upset.

How could he plan to be halfway across the world and not discuss it with her? What did that say about their relationship? And what did it say about *him* to put things in motion without considering how his absence and the potential danger he'd be in would affect her peace of mind?

After thinking about the limited time they might have together, she packed her satchel, borrowed her uncle's Audi and now stood outside Kingston's door, knocking.

A moment later Kingston opened it, wearing sweatpants and a tee-shirt he was in the process of pulling on. His gaze grew wary and he grimaced but said nothing. He stepped back and allowed her to go past him, then closed the door.

The atmosphere inside the apartment was cool and the uncluttered space was neat. Kingston was tidy, while she made herself comfortable wherever she went, by spreading her possessions around.

His laptop was open on a table at the far end of the living room, where light flooded through the wall of glass facing the street.

She dropped her computer bag and leather satchel on the sofa and stood in front of Kingston.

When he didn't say a word, Sam slid her arms around him and spoke softly into his shirt. "I'm sorry. I was being …"

"Sam," he finished, pushing the hair away from her brow to reveal her eyes. "You were just being yourself."

Shrugging, she said, "Right, but I don't want anything to happen to you."

"I'm careful when I travel to do a story," he countered. "You know that."

She stepped back, propped both hands on her hips and looked him up and down. "Is that so? Remember when you went to Yemen?"

Kingston folded both arms across his chest and leaned toward her. "I came back in one piece, didn't I?"

"But you were caught in that crossfire and then that building next door to you was bombed." Sam's voice grew urgent and revealed how concerned she was, so she drew a calming breath. "And for two days, nobody knew whether you were dead or alive." Her sentence ended in a whisper. "I couldn't eat, I couldn't sleep. I—I needed to know where you were. The silence was frightening."

Her concerns became background noise the moment his eyes glazed over, as if his memories from that experience had resurfaced. What she knew was only half of what he'd endured during those out-of-touch times. Some things he kept to himself. His blank expression gave no indication of what he was thinking, but she had a painful flashback.

For several months after Kingston's return, she'd held him close each night as he descended into hell. She was at risk from his flailing limbs. Morning after morning, she woke sore and exhausted. Kingston thrashed and yelled in her arms until he was hoarse. Clinging to him as if he were a lifeline, she whispered soothing words until he was at peace.

When his eyes opened and clarity returned, Kingston thanked her with soft kisses. He'd never disclosed the horrors that came to him at night. In fact, he'd begged her not to sleep in his bed for fear of harming her, but she refused to be anywhere else.

That thought brought back her annoyance with him. The pandemic had made her comfortable with having him in proximity. Now, he was planning a separation without telling her.

"Kingston." Sam's next words were harsher than intended. "Are you listening to me?"

Her commanding tone lifted the haze he'd entered. His jaw hardened. "This situation is different."

She stifled the urge to sock him in the jaw. "But you'll still be at risk."

Kingston stepped in closer and held her by both arms, and she figured he'd switch gears. "I'm glad you came over. You know all my ins and outs and I can't resist you, especially since you've been giving me the silent treatment."

She looked away, a little ashamed. Kingston had the power to make her examine herself and know she could do better. He was always patient, even in this situation when she was being petty.

He smiled, then released her. "So, are you going to tell me why you're here? I know you didn't come because you forgave me."

"There's nothing to forgive, except the fact that you want what you want and aren't willing to hear my side." She sighed and threw her head back. Several seconds ticked by before she said, "All I know is that if you go, I'll be on pins and needles until you return."

His slow smile and the light in his eyes spoke of discovery. Kingston didn't say what he'd found out, but the satisfaction in his gaze made her want to avoid connecting with him, and that was unlike her. Sam faced everything head on, except for the part where she avoided thinking about where their relationship was heading. Sometimes, it was easier to go with the flow and let things develop on their own.

Kingston tipped her chin up with one finger and kissed the side of her mouth. "I know you care, and that's important to me. But aside from that, tell me what's up?"

She didn't want to talk about work this minute, so she clasped his head with both hands and kissed him. Kingston's mouth opened and when his tongue made contact with hers, Sam relished everything about this man who touched the deepest parts of her with his love. Kingston knew her body, mind, and soul. His hands slid around her waist and pulled her closer. Thoughts of work flew further away and as his fingers spread across her back, she melted into him. This was where she wanted and needed to be.

A muted buzzing brought her back to reality. "I have to get that," she murmured.

Kingston released her and she sat on a nearby recliner and pulled the cell phone out of her bag. Seeing the familiar name on her Caller ID, she mouthed, "It's my supervisor," before pressing the answer icon. "Yes, Catherine."

"What progress have you made with your interviews?"

The abrupt question and tone didn't phase Sam. Catherine was a no-nonsense woman who didn't waste words.

"I still have a few more to do—"

"I'm not sure whose toes you've stepped on, but I got a call about you turning over a few rocks. I allow you to do some of the stories you choose because you have a nose for what makes great news, but—"

"Please don't tell me you're calling to say I'm to abandon this story."

"I'm not saying that." She rebutted. "Yet. We both know that when things like this happen, it means there's something someone wants to keep hidden. What I *am* saying is that you should be careful."

Catherine's words jarred Sam, who rolled her shoulders. She moved the phone to her other ear and stared at Kingston, who walked into the kitchen. He pulled a bottle of water from the fridge and tipped his head back to drink. Everything about him was fine. From his handsome features, muscular physique, to his casual air of confidence. Kingston was all man. Too much for her family, but all man.

Her mind came back to business when Catherine said, "Don't neglect the story about that brilliant teenager with autism. Your deadline is coming up fast."

"I won't, and I'll keep my eyes open. See you next week."

"Sam, I need to hear from you more often," Catherine warned. "Keep me updated on the vaccine story."

Nodding as if Catherine stood in the room, she answered, "We'll talk more about it when we meet."

Frowning, and now suspicious, Sam ended the call. Catherine's words, combined with Ted's behaviour made her skin prickle. She understood that not all altruistic gestures came from a place of pure-heartedness. Sometimes, people gave for the benefit of making themselves feel better, others did it for the publicity angle, but she couldn't see through knowing a product could have dangerous effects on the human body and still administering it to unsuspecting people. It didn't make sense for a business organization. The bad publicity could bring down a company, so the risk wasn't worth taking.

What am I missing?

When she looked up, Kingston had returned and stood gazing at her.

"I need your help," she said.

Kingston's work connections gave him access to information she didn't have, which was why she'd come to see him. Aside from the fact that she was over her snit.

He guided her from the recliner to the sofa and settled on the cushion next to her. "Sure. What do you need?"

Sam explained what she was looking for and gave him the names of the people whose business dealings piqued her interest. While she spoke, Kingston rubbed his jaw and kept his attention focused on her. The only sound and movement in the room came from the ticking and the pendulum in the grandfather clock across the room.

When their eyes met, Kingston's were narrowed. "These are important people. We may raise red flags trying to find out the level of their involvement in this."

She pushed one hand through her hair and shook her head. "That's never been an issue when you're working on your own stories."

"Maybe not, but mine usually stem from the things people do out in the open. Not the things they want to keep under wraps. The skeletons they want to keep stacked in the closet."

"I understand all of that," she shot back, "but you will arouse less suspicion than I will stumbling around to get the data I need."

He ran the pad of his thumb across the back of her hand. "Let me access the company library and make some calls. If there's anything that's not on the level, I'll know after that."

Kingston took several steps toward his laptop then stopped short. "I have another idea."

"What is it?" Sam's curiosity rose, as it usually did whenever Kingston began a discussion with those words.

"Wouldn't you get further if you brought in Evita? With her being a nurse with that outfit … What is it?"

Releasing her breath on a sigh, Sam said, "Doctors Who Care Worldwide."

"Yes, that's it." Snapping his fingers, he added, "She might know something."

Evita had been overseas for some time working for a network of doctors who provided their services free of charge in several West African countries. Why Evita chose to work so far from home was a mystery to Sam, but she'd seemed resolute about going during their last conversation.

When Kingston's words unraveled in her brain, Sam's eyes widened. "Absolutely not!"

"But she's also your best friend. At least that's what you told me. What's changed?" He watched her as if puzzled because she never dismissed his ideas.

"I'm just being cautious," she offered.

"Aren't you the one who's always saying, 'Let bygones be bygones?'"

"And, aren't you the one who just warned me to be careful with digging up information?"

"Yes, but—"

"Then let sleeping dogs lie," she snapped. "I don't need her."

Chapter 5

"All of this close attention is liable to give me a big head." Kingston wriggled his eyebrows while staring into Sam's eyes. "But the reality is that you're waiting to pounce."

"We don't have a lot of time, so I want to get all the information I can while you're here with me."

He reached across the table and laid a hand on hers. "I get it. But watching me work is not going to help me retrieve the data I need any faster."

"I know, but considering the people involved, I almost feel like …"

When she didn't continue, he said, "You think what you're looking for will disappear?"

Sighing, she pulled her hand out of reach. "Yes. Something about this doesn't sit right with me, and there are missing pieces."

"How do you know?"

"My gut tells me. It always does. Aside from that, Ted is hiding something."

His gaze went back to the laptop screen and he ran one finger over the glass.

"What is it?" she asked.

"Nothing yet."

She hunched over the table's polished surface. "You don't get that serious look unless you find something that doesn't add up."

"That would be all the time in my line of work," he quipped. "Let's go out and get some air and do lunch."

"Where did that come from?" She swirled a lock of hair around her fingers. "Are you trying to distract me?"

Kingston tipped one brow. "Is it working?"

"Of course not."

Sam scattered his thoughts when she swept her hair into a ponytail, tightening the shirt across her breasts.

"Anyway. I was serious." He waved toward her satchel and made as if to rise. "I'm sure you have a tube of lipstick in your bag or something. Go put some on while I grab my wallet."

"I'm good with this diversion, although I haven't forgotten."

With a quirk to his lips, Kingston said, "Of course you wouldn't. Be patient."

She sniffed, then flounced away, which made him chuckle. Sam was expert at being a drama queen, but Kingston knew what many didn't. She could be a 'Princess' and not feel guilty when she was at home with her family. To others she probably seemed spoiled, coming from prominent and wealthy parents. But Sam didn't make a practice of always trying to get her own way. Maneuvering between both personas was necessary, especially in the working world.

After searching her bag, Sam entered his bedroom.

A second later, Kingston picked up his cell phone and dialed a friend's number.

"KC, good to hear from you." Dr. Maxwell William's booming voice forced Kingston to pull the phone away from his ear. He sounded as robust as his linebacker's frame. "What's up?"

"I'm doing some research for an article and came across something curious." He glanced over his shoulder as he walked across the room. "Vaccines, from what I know, they take somewhere between ten to twelve years to develop."

"That's a fact. Sometimes longer."

"So, in your view, if a new vaccine was developed for something like Ebola …"

"Put it this way, a lot of studies have already been done on the virus and vaccines produced—"

Rubbing the back of his neck, Kingston asked, "But what if a company fast-tracked their own vaccine with a view to distributing it at cheaper rates to poor countries?"

"It's a way to make money. Let's face it, there's a lot of competition in the pharmaceutical industry." He cleared his throat, then asked, "Why the interest? Are you working on a story?"

Glancing over his shoulder, Kingston said, "Yes and no."

Max laughed. "You are as cagey as ever. How are you going to ask me questions and won't answer the single one I'm asking."

"You know how it is. Can't release too many details while I'm pulling the facts together."

"Don't I know it." Maxwell had previously worked as part of a research team on developing cannabis for various uses. These days, he also wrote for medical journals. Their friendship went back to New York University and their work in the media kept them connected. Even if they didn't hear from each other in months, they easily picked up the thread of their relationship once they were back in contact.

"What do you know about George Belnavis and Bronson Hardy?" Kingston asked, his tone casual.

"If I recall correctly, both are shareholders in a company called Mi-Vaxx. They produce vaccines."

Kingston went to the sofa near the widescreen, fifty-five-inch television and straightened the cushions while listening. "Right."

"Mind telling me why you're looking at them?" Max asked, "Although I can guess."

Kingston walked toward the windows that faced the street and kept his voice low. "Same article."

"Got it, but I know how deep your stories go."

Chuckling, Kingston beckoned to Sam who appeared then. "Don't read more into it than what is there."

"Whatever you say. Always good to hear from you. Call me if you need anything more."

"Thanks. I will." He ended the call and hugged Sam, then whispered in her ear. "You look pretty."

Her cheeks flushed and she batted her eyelashes playfully. "You're making me hot and bothered."

Kingston's lips lifted at the corners as he placed the phone on the center table. "When that stops, I'd say it's time for us to part company."

Sam tipped her head back and raised her brows. "You expect the heat between us to stay the same after five, ten, fifteen years?"

His hands slid up to her shoulders. "It will, if we keep stoking the fire."

She smiled, a smug gesture. "Sounds like you have long-term plans."

"I'd be a fool to let you get away." He stroked her cheek then turned toward the bedroom. "I'll be back in a minute."

"Sure. Don't keep me waiting too long."

Backing away, he said, "I won't, she-who-loves-to-chew."

Sam's smile was nothing short of brilliant. "No more than you do, my love."

Her indulgent tone reminded him of how well they fit together. Sam was supportive, understood his quirks, and they shared common interests—books, food, movies. While stepping into his jeans, Kingston asked himself why he hadn't yet asked Sam to be his wife.

Likely because of her family. From the little she'd said before they visited Jamaica, he understood what she finally told him when they touched down on the island. Her family wouldn't approve of him.

After meeting them, Kingston's instincts told him that even if he proposed, she wouldn't say yes at this point. And he didn't blame her. Family and marriage were lifelong commitments. He wouldn't go into the latter without knowing he was making the right decision.

Truth be told, his parents were not enthusiastic about Sam, but nowhere near as rude as hers had been. His mother's reaction to meeting Sam was unexpected. Her reservations over Sam's appearance and social status shocked him. JoAnne Coburn had gone through the same struggles with her people over marrying his father. Kingston hadn't made a fuss over their lack of warmth, but knew he'd address that matter in time. His thoughts returned to the conversation with Sam two days ago and the room faded.

He was back to that night when hell exploded in North Korea. Kingston and another journalist, Antonio Perez, who insisted upon going, weren't supposed to be there. He'd had a brainwave and decided to take a chance on getting a huge story surrounding several American businessmen, who had been kidnapped and were being held for ransom. Their presence and existence were denied by the dictator—a short, stubby wanna-be demon.

Going on instinct because he had a strong nose for explosive stories, Kingston accessed most of the funds he'd been given to cover his expenses for two previous trips and this one and prepared for whatever would unfold.

Kingston and Perez spent two exhausting days trekking through a forest to reach the designated area where they would meet their informant. With them, they carried twenty-thousand American dollars to exchange for the prized information they sought.

Instead, treachery had reached the location first. They walked into the small clearing to find that rigor mortis had begun its assault upon their informant's body.

Kingston immediately knew the identity by the remnants of clothing which were to be worn by the-man-with-no-name. Although the body was in a kneeling position and face-down, Kingston had seen enough of the dead to know the corpse hadn't been there for long. The smell of decay hadn't yet settled or spread to the animals and insects.

After scanning the area, he placed a finger against his lips to silence Antonio, then whispered, "He was killed right here."

He crouched to get a better look without moving closer. The deceased was frozen in the position of assault. The man had been brutally sodomized and knifed in the back.

Slowly, Kingston rose to his feet and stood transfixed until he heard voices that were coming closer. Only Antonio's previous stealth training in the army and Kingston's knowledge of the area saved them. Another three days went by before they emerged from the forest, having encountered people from several villages, and leaving the armed men behind.

Bartering with the money they carried ensured their safety. They didn't have enough left to buy a hotdog by the time they reached the South Korean border. Their wits and connections through their respective papers ensured they returned home safely.

That was before he re-connected with Sam. The truth was, the adventure of being on the ground to track a story that mattered still called to him, but knowing she was waiting for him made a difference. His China trip might have to go on hold based on everything that was happening around them.

When he looked up, Sam stood in the doorway to the bedroom. The olive hue to her skin had fled, leaving her face colorless. She remained silent, but her eyes were huge.

"What's the matter, hon?"

"Change in plans." Sam smoothed her hair then hunched as if cold, sure signs that she was nervous. "Ted just called and asked that I meet him for lunch."

Kingston pulled down his shirt, frowning. "So why do you look as if you got bad news."

"He refused to say anything on the phone." She came toward him, her expression perplexed. "He's in more trouble than I thought."

"Why d'you think that?"

"Ted sounded weird and flustered, and he was whispering as if he didn't want anyone to hear his conversation. He sounded as if something bad happened."

Chapter 6

"Are you going to tell me what's really going on?" Sam asked.

Ted's troubled expression tugged at her heart because she'd never seen him like this before. His hand shook while he tapped a restless drumbeat on the wooden table. What made her more curious was that he met them downtown at Miss Mabel's Jamaican Joint. Ted didn't eat at places like the mom and pop establishment where they now sat. His taste ran more to expensive restaurants that catered to Chicago's wealthy residents. Not to say he didn't enjoy Jamaican home cooking. The restaurant he'd sent them to was a testament to that. For Ted, everything had its time and place.

"I don't know where to start." Against his black shirt, Ted's skin was washed out and his face drawn. When his gaze flicked to the doorway, she understood part of his concern.

"He's parking the car."

A chiding note laced Ted's voice. "I wanted to have a confidential conversation with you. "

"I know, and I'm sorry." She laid her hand over his and squeezed. "But I suspected it might have to do with whatever was bothering you when we spoke the other day."

Ted looked beyond her, then asked, "And that's why you brought him?"

She glanced at the group of men who went past them and sat a few tables away. "I don't like the tone of that *him*."

"I don't share your parents' prejudices," he snapped.

Looking him straight in the eyes, she said, "I was just making sure."

"I should apologize." He ran one hand over his hair. "I'm sorry. Trust me, I have more to worry about than who you're seeing."

He had met Kingston previously, but they had not had a proper conversation. At the time, Kingston had given her a ride to meet Ted, then left for an interview and she hadn't explained who he was. She'd been strangely reluctant to share Kingston's role in her life with Ted, but he'd been wise enough to figure out what she hadn't said. Now, she pulled in a breath and smiled faintly. "I trust Kingston with my life."

"He must be quite a man to earn your trust, considering …"

"I apologize for bringing him into this situation with us, but the truth is, he'll be helping with my research," she said, "He's one of the good ones."

They both knew she'd struggled with choosing her close associates because of her history in Jamaica. Back home, people assumed she was snooty because of the color of her skin and were suspicious of her. In school, Sam didn't have many friends until the other girls realized she wasn't stuck up.

When Sam's parents allowed her to finish her schooling in New York, she had difficulty coping, but meeting Evita made her life bearable. Both girls were relieved and elated to find out they were from the same place, despite their different backgrounds. A stupid argument over Evita breaking up with Trey-Jon because her parents wanted her dating a doctor instead of a techie had escalated until their friendship cooled. They drifted apart and didn't speak for an extended time. The next contact between them came when Evita announced she'd be moving overseas for work. Now and then, they exchanged greetings via social media.

The ping that came from cutlery snapped Sam from her memories and she looked up when Kingston stood next to the table. He pulled out a chair and greeted Ted.

While they chatted, Sam admired Kingston's ability to put people at ease, which was an advantage in their line of work.

"Why did you choose this place?" Sam asked when the waiter brought their drinks and left. Ted asked him to come back in five minutes with a menu. "Especially since I'm staying with you. What was so important?"

"You weren't around when this matter came up. Plus, I'm not likely to run into anyone I know here." Smiling faintly, he continued, "Except maybe one of my lawyers, who likes their food."

His answer didn't surprise her. "I figured that was at least one of your reasons."

She slid the glass of soda water to Kingston, but not before taking a sip. His lips quirked when their eyes met. Their running joke was that if someone had it in for him and tried to poison him, she'd be the first victim. Although she didn't always intend to, she also sampled his meals before he got a taste.

When her uncle's gaze moved between Kingston and her, Sam gave him a slight nod. Her intention was to show him the regard she had for this man, who accepted her with all the peculiarities that went with her character. The same way she accepted him.

Her mind flashed back to her phone conversation with Michele, who had given Kingston the name Caramel King, in homage to his name and complexion. She had no issues with Kingston. Pity their parents weren't as enlightened.

Sam put her thoughts on hold when Ted pulled out his phone, scrolled for a bit, then handed it to her. She read the messages, with her heart fluttering as she opened each one. Her uncle was being blackmailed. The moment her gaze jumped to his, Sam asked, "Have you paid this person anything?"

After shaking his head, Ted smiled. "You know how I feel about throwing away money."

Kingston didn't ask what they were talking about, but the slight angling of his head toward Sam confirmed he was listening. She filled him in with two sentences, then said, "This doesn't look good. They make it sound as if the company knows their product isn't doing what it's supposed to." She gave the phone back to Ted. "And whoever sent you those messages are well aware. But why you?"

With a shrug and a faint smile, he said, "Maybe they did eeny meeny miney mo from a list of names or they figure I can meet their demands because of my connection to The Castle."

"There is that."

"If you don't mind me asking, how much do you know about the drug they're blackmailing you over?" Kingston asked.

"It protects against the Ebola virus and has an eighty-five percent efficacy rate, pretty much like the ones used to combat today's scourge."

"I see." Kingston rested both arms on the table and leaned in closer. "How long did it take to develop?"

After a sip of water, Ted set his glass down carefully and cleared his throat. "Four years."

For Sam, that disclosure raised faint alarm bells. That was a short period of time to develop effective medication against such a deadly virus. Her discomfort was reflected on Kingston's face. "That sounds like indecent haste to me."

"It's a deadly virus." Ted opened both hands. "The team at MiVaxx was doing their best to come up with solutions. They expected a new outbreak, which did happen earlier this year."

"Understood, but who's trying to get money from you and why?"

Rubbing his forehead, Ted admitted, "They threatened to leak news of the effect the drug had during clinical trials. They're also insinuating that there are other serious side effects."

"Like what?" Kingston asked before Sam could open her mouth.

Sinking in his seat, Ted sighed. "I didn't ask because I don't think it's wise to engage them."

"Have you contacted MiVaxx?" Sam asked, frowning.

Ted's attention shifted to the people sitting around them, who seemed immersed in their meals and conversation, then returned to Sam. "Yes, and I sent the previous email to the tech division of their security department."

"The fact that they've contacted you again tells me MiVaxx hasn't found out where the first message originated."

"Unfortunately not, and the text that came in yesterday was traced to a burner phone."

With one hand, Sam swept the hair off her face. "D'you have any kind of plan to deal with this situation if it goes any further?"

Ted leaned on one elbow and looked at his watch. "Other than using my own resources to try and track these criminals, there's not much else I can do, is there?"

"There may be something." Kingston met Sam's gaze, then Ted's. "I have an idea. Give me an hour, but it's going to mean we have to abandon lunch."

"That's definitely not a problem," Ted said, pumping Kingston's hand in gratitude. "I'm thankful for anything that may help before things get dicey."

Kingston's expression was serious when he replied, "There are no guarantees, but I'll do my best to help you get some clarity."

Chapter 7

Trey-Jon released a long, low whistle when he looked up from the screen. "I'd like to enjoy boring things like sitting on a porch in my old age with the woman who eventually becomes my wife and the mother of my children."

"And there's no reason you shouldn't be able to enjoy that." Kingston perched on the side of the desk his friend occupied.

Trey-Jon Witter was another pal from the university, but his life revolved around the dark web under the guise of creating gaming software. Kingston didn't know exactly what he did and who employed him. All he was certain of was that whenever he needed information he couldn't find anywhere, Trey-Jon was guaranteed to help without creating any ripples.

"Riiight." Trey-Jon dragged out the word in a derisive way. "I never mastered enough biology in pre-med for the big wigs to be involved in this stuff you have me snooping into." Trey-Jon's gaze cut to him. "You're always searching for stuff nobody should even be looking at."

Kingston stood and slid both hands into his pockets. "Which is why

I know I've come to the right place."

They both focused on the notepaper Kingston had laid next to Trey-Jon's keyboard.

"So, what exactly am I looking for?" he asked, running a hand over his cornrows.

"I'm really not sure, but Belnavis would be a good start."

Trey-Jon spun his chair around to face another computer. He tapped a pen rhythmically on the mouse pad and stared at the screen. "Why him?"

"Just a feeling I have and what I know of him." Kingston shrugged. "He's supposed to be an upstanding businessman, mega-rich and all that, but his name always pops up in connection with some shady business."

"Like what?"

"This, for instance. And there was the scandal the other day with that politician who was involved in offshore banking and tax evasion."

Trey-Jon looked at him sideways and finger-combed his beard. "Like I said, the stuff you're always interested in ..."

They both chuckled, then Trey-Jon turned back to the keyboard and pulled himself toward the desk. When Kingston didn't move out of range, he gave him an inquiring look.

"What's the matter?" Kingston asked.

"You're forgetting the rules. I'm not doing this with you looking over my shoulder. If you stay there, I might have to kill you afterward."

"Whatever man." Kingston marched to the other side of the desk and plopped down into a rocking chair that didn't fit the sparse furnishings in Trey-Jon's home. During his talk with Sam's uncle, he remembered that Trey-Jon lived in Chicago. A phone call was enough to bring Kingston here, but he left Sam at the apartment before making the trip across town. She hadn't been happy with the arrangements but understood his position. The less she knew, the better.

"So, you want me to go down this list?"

"Uh-huh." Kingston dipped his head twice, which set the chair in motion.

"What am I getting in return?"

Chuckling, Kingston said, "Name your price."

Trey-Jon sucked his teeth and tipped his chin toward the bags of Chinese food Kingston had placed on his kitchen counter. "All you're likely to give me is a heart attack from that fast food."

"For which you'd sell one of your relatives."

They shared a hearty laugh. Trey-Jon's love for Chinese food was legendary and that hadn't changed since their university days.

"The least you can do is make me a plate while I do your dirty work."

"Your wish is currently my command." Kingston walked into the compact kitchen and rifled through the bags, lifting out several boxes. He'd bought cashew chicken, roast pork, beef curry, fried rice, and a serving of noodles. His friend would have food for days and it was simply Kingston's way of showing appreciation for his expertise.

Despite having his two-bedroom apartment crowded with several computers and surge protectors, overlapping electrical cords, and a huge top-of-the-line Multifunction Xerox printer, Trey-Jon didn't need anything Kingston could provide. He made good money, but had always been frugal, except when it came to his tech business. He would never try to snoop on the cheap.

"Bring a beer while you're at it," Trey-Jon called.

"No problem." Kingston opened the fridge and couldn't help laughing. Since he introduced Trey-Jon to Red Stripe Beer, he hadn't stopped drinking it. He washed the top of the cans, dried them, then handed one to Trey-Jon and popped the other for himself.

"Did I give you permission to drink any of my stuff?" Trey-Jon's serious expression gave way to a grin. "Coming up in my home and sucking down my beer like you helped me buy it."

"The food is compensation," Kingston said as he lowered himself into the rocking chair.

"Wrong. That's for people's business you have me digging through."

"Next time, I'll be sure to bring a six-pack."

"You better," Trey-Jon grumbled, then turned a hard gaze on him. "You want to tell me what this information is for?"

"Sam is working on a story." He placed the can on the tile, preparing to rise. "These men are connected to the company she's researching."

"Interesting people." Trey-Jon's warning glance reminded Kingston to stay on the other side of the desk. "The first two I've looked at have certain things in common." After swallowing several mouthfuls of beer, he continued. "Offshore banking. Local and overseas investments."

"Where?" Kingston asked. "The investments, I mean."

"The place they have in common is Liberia."

"Oh?" From what Kingston remembered, Liberia was one of the West African countries affected by the Ebola virus during the outbreak several years ago. That country, and others in a similar position, would have been ripe for the dumping of inferior drugs as it struggled to survive in a world of rapidly changing variants of deadly viruses and other diseases.

Pacing in front of several large computer screens, Kingston searched his mind for what he remembered about that time. He was about to ask Trey-Jon to do a search on MiVaxx when his phone buzzed. A glance confirmed that Sam was calling.

"Yeah, hon. All is well?"

"Most things." She inhaled, and Kingston didn't know what to expect.

"On his way back to The Castle, Ted received another message."

Kingston walked to the window and peered into the street. "What did they say this time?"

"They threatened to release a story to the media if he doesn't pay up by end of day tomorrow."

He stayed quiet, instinctively. Something else was coming.

"The message hinted that he'd also be in physical danger."

Massaging his temples, Kingston asked, "What does he plan to do about his security?"

"He's getting a bodyguard."

"Sounds good." Sam had called him because she was rattled. The tightness to her voice clued him in, so he said, "I'll be with you as soon as I'm finished here, which should be inside an hour."

The moment he hung up the phone, Trey-Jon tipped his brow. "You won't leave here with some of that information. I'm an IT professional, not a magician."

Kingston chuckled and picked up his beer. "I'm perfectly aware of that. While you're at it, I'd like to add one more individual to that list."

"Since you're going for broke, just go right ahead." Trey-Jon pushed the paper toward Kingston, who scrawled another name on the bottom of the sheet.

Chapter 8

"Why is today the first time I'm hearing about this deal?"

The man who'd been introduced as Shastra "Shaz" Bostwick slid into a seat and placed a glass of water on the conference table. His honey-gold skin, well-groomed locs, and goatee, plus his immaculate gray suit commanded attention.

If Sam was single, she'd certainly have given him a second look. Maybe a third. Her parents would definitely have liked him better with his expensive suit than Kingston—except for those long shiny locs. They loved Jamaica, but not all things Jamaican.

"The company used their lawyers," Ted answered in a strangled voice. "It was easier, and since they insisted it was expedient to have the contract signed, we met and …" He folded both hands on the table and didn't finish his sentence.

Tapping his pen on the wooden surface, Shaz said, "Sounds like they needed their investors' money and signatures at an ungodly speed."

Jaidev Maharaj, a handsome East Indian man, who practised holistic medicine in the States and in the Middle Eastern country of Durabia, focused on Ted. "It didn't strike you as indecent, the haste with which MiVaxx needed your cash?"

"They mentioned additional research, which was where they needed the investment dollars. A friend of mine was already on the board, and he endorsed the move. Plus, they guaranteed a return on our investment and had come through before, so it wasn't a hard decision to make."

The dark-haired man, Daron Kincaid, who hadn't yet weighed in on the conversation, cleared his throat. "And look where that got you."

Sam exchanged a glance with Kingston, who arrived several minutes ago. She'd called him while en route to let him know Ted had sent another vehicle to escort her to The Castle. He hadn't given her a reason, but she had her suspicions. The hefty man, who drove ahead of the Audi, couldn't be anything but a security guard. On her way over, she'd noticed the dark clouds that had gathered in what had been a clear sky moments before. Another bad sign.

A glance at her uncle had Sam concerned all over again. If it were possible, she'd think he lost weight overnight. As soon as they left this meeting, and had a moment's privacy, she'd ask him some questions.

Kingston laid one hand on top of hers. His calming touch stilled her movement. She'd been drumming on her leg, agitated simply by looking at Ted. He wasn't telling her everything. Their eyes met, and he gave her a reassuring smile, which left as soon as his gaze slid back to Shaz, who she gathered was one of his lawyers.

"So, pertaining to your security concerns," Daron said, laying a phone on the surface of the semi-circular table. "You can get rid of the man outside the door as soon as we're finished here. We'll use my team of experts. They are people I trust with my life."

Alejandro Reyes, or Dro, a dark-haired man with intense eyes nodded. "That's an excellent move."

"Sam is staying with her uncle and she'll be here for another day or so. Also, she will be out and about with me. How do you propose to handle that?" Kingston asked.

"I can assign a security team to her, as well," Daron replied. "That won't be a problem."

She wanted to protest that nobody was after her, but something held her back. Her uncle's secrets meant she couldn't take anything for granted.

Kingston nodded. "Sounds good."

"I'm going to need your phone," Daron said, holding out one hand.

Sighing, Ted reached into the pocket of his jacket and gave it to Daron. "What are you doing?"

As he powered down the cellular and slid it open, Daron said, "Just adding a little something that will trip a recording device once an unknown number connects to your phone."

"That's some high-tech stuff," Kingston said, raising one brow.

Getting to his feet, Shaz chuckled. "You don't know the half of it."

At that moment, two females in uniforms entered the room and arranged several trays of refreshment on a sideboard.

"Your timing is perfect, as always," Jai said, while Shaz sauntered to where the food was laid out.

"Would you like anything?" Shaz asked, his gaze moving between Sam and Kingston.

"I could use a little something," Kingston said, "I missed lunch."

"Feel free." Jai waved toward where Shaz stood as Kingston rose. "We have healthy menu items, and there's the stuff Shaz likes."

Over his shoulder, Shaz retorted, "Go on acting as if you don't indulge now and then."

"Certainly nowhere as often as you."

"Don't listen to him," Shaz said, then bit into a cocktail patty. "Actually, let me amend that. He's a distinguished doctor, excellent at what he does. But when a man is hungry, he needs filling food and not the stuff that disappears as soon as you swallow it."

Dro grinned while Shaz continued to fill a small plate with items from the silver trays. "Be sure to have some patties. They are good."

"Thanks for the recommendation." Kingston selected a few items, picked up a napkin and fork, and offered the plate to Sam before he reclaimed his seat.

She gave him a grateful smile and bit into a patty.

"Good?" Kingston asked, while she chewed.

Nodding slowly, Sam savored the flaky crust and spicy mincemeat she hadn't indulged in, in ages.

Kingston sampled another one while Daron turned the phone back on and handed it to Ted, who studied it as if it would bite.

"Thanks, you did say it would only record calls from unknown numbers, right?"

"Yes. That's the extent to which my team will be invading your privacy." Every bit of amusement left Daron's face when he asked, "What time did the caller say he'd be ringing you back this evening?"

"Five o' clock." Ted ran one hand through his hair, then brushed back the strands left standing on end.

"Two hours from now," Kingston said, glancing at his watch.

"And you did say he'd be calling with instructions for you to meet him?" Daron asked.

Ted nodded, his complexion ashen.

His condition worried Sam and the patty sat like lead in her stomach. But he'd reassured her that the group of men he was meeting were well-equipped and would know what to do. That's why he insisted on her coming here.

"Is there something you're not telling us?" Jai asked, studying Ted. "You don't look so good."

He swallowed as if the effort was almost beyond him, then cleared his throat.

When Sam met his worried gaze, her scalp prickled. Ted was looking at her as if she'd been diagnosed with a terminal disease.

Nobody in the room moved, until Kingston's husky voice broke the silence. "Don't tell me they threatened Sam, too?"

Chapter 9

"Dude knows more than he's telling you." Trey-Jon sounded preoccupied, the way he did when something on the screen had his full attention.

"What makes you think that?" Kingston asked, pacing the sidewalk at the front of The Castle. He looked over his shoulder to be sure he was alone. After he realized what the Kings he'd been introduced to were capable of doing, he thought it best to make this call in the open air. His mind was not at ease, but Sam was safe with a security guard posted outside the door of her uncle's suite. The Kings had promised their new guard would meet them at the suite and had delivered on that.

Although he'd come directly from the conference room and Sam had gone straight back to the suite, Kingston still had a niggle of uneasiness. The sooner he could return to her side, the better he'd feel.

Trey-Jon's answer disturbed Kingston's thoughts. "He's close with one of the investors, and they go way back."

Strolling farther from the building, Kingston scanned his surroundings.

The men had insisted that all of them stay at The Castle while they organized a safe escort for Ted to the meeting location. Since Sam was under threat, Kingston had no problem remaining where she would be safe.

"He did say he put money on the table because an associate of his thought it was a good deal."

"I believe that would be Bronson Hardy. On the surface, he seems upstanding, like that other guy Belnavis." The clatter of the keyboard interrupted his words. "But Hardy's night-time activity makes me think he's King of the Dancehall or something."

"I see you're trying to take Beenie Man's title," Kingston said, in reference to one of Jamaica's most popular deejays from the 80s and 90s.

"Nah, he has the undisputed title." Trey-Jon sucked in a deep breath then continued, "This man seems to make it his life's work to find shady causes to put his money into, including a string of nightclubs. Based on the young women he surrounds himself with, I'd say he also doesn't believe in staying within his age group. I wouldn't be surprised to learn he's a heavy investor in not only the manufacturing of Viagra. There's a little pink pill for the ladies, too."

"I doubt that," Kingston scratched his head, distracted by the unexpected information Trey-Jon threw at him. He could be a joker at times.

"Ya don't know everything, I'm suggesting that you get out more without it being drama and politics. As I was saying, it was a female who discovered the pink pill for women. She called it Addyl ..."

"I remember that story," Kingston said, touching his forehead. "She sold the company for one billion dollars to the embattled big Pharma when they needed to showcase the next big thing. Big Pharma's situation got worse and she managed to get her pink pill company back for little to nothing. Word is she almost got it back for free. So, don't tell me ..."

"Yes sir, your Mister Bronson Hardy has tossed a wad of money into the manufacturing of the mood and sex elevation business for quite some time. Word is, he also uses it to keep the women in his nightclub eager and available for hefty fees."

"Is the information on Bronson so sensitive you can't send it in an email?" Kingston asked.

"My desire to live supersedes our friendship, buddy. But tonight, I'm feeling generous."

Chuckling, Kingston shook his head. "If I know you well, you'll send me a document with a complicated password that'll take me five attempts to get it right."

"It's all a part of my brilliance, bro."

"Right." Scanning the area, Kingston asked, "So aside from Hardy's love life and these other shenanigans, what else makes him special?"

"Most of his money is shipped out of the country as soon as he can shuffle it around long enough to make it disappear."

"He's not the only one who operates in that way." Staring at the BMW pulling into the driveway, Kingston added, "High rollers always cover their behinds for when Uncle Sam catches up with them."

"His name has come up in relation to three or four dodgy medications that are under investigation. These are the same ones shipped to third-world countries that can't afford to buy top-of-the-line products and end up with questionable medicine that may or may not be approved by the Food and Drug Administration."

"So, you think he deliberately finds a particular kind of product that's made available to a specific demographic, knowing full well that they might cause harm?"

"Looks that way to me." The crackle of paper accompanied Trey-Jon's words. "I'm looking at maybe half a dozen drugs that people have sued these companies for that have caused adverse effects, including death."

"I wouldn't use that word to describe something as final as passing from this earth. That's more of a catastrophe."

"Yeah, well, in my book if kicking the bucket isn't an adverse reaction to a drug, I don't know what is."

His comment made Kingston chuckle. "Whatever man, but these guys are something else. It's as if the more money they have, the less their conscience troubles them."

"Some would say, the more money you have, the more you crave."

"Facts." His stomach turned over as he asked, "So about her uncle …"

"He's in deep, moneywise. I think it's a case of what we were just speaking about. He invested in a good thing and just wanted a big return on the cash he put in. There's a pattern though."

"What d'you mean?"

"Same as his friend. Some dicey projects he should have avoided getting involved in."

"Is there any indication that …" Kingston looked up and frowned as a sudden burst of raindrops rushed to meet the ground. An Audi, identical to the one that belonged to Ted, swept out of the parking lot and down the driveway. But it couldn't be his because Ted was safely closeted with Sam upstairs.

"Are you asking me if I think he's dirty?"

Working a kink out of his neck, Kingston sighed. "I guess."

"I wouldn't want to be in the awkward situation you're in, especially if your woman finds out you're digging into her family's business."

"Yeah, there's that." For no reason Kingston could fathom, goose-bumps covered his skin. "I have to go. I'd appreciate it if you'd see if there's anything else I need to know about these investments, or something else that might be important."

"I will. By the way, I discovered that aside from the Kings and Knights, The Castle also has a set of Queens, one of which is your darling Sam. Or, at least, she's primed to be in some excellent company. So, a little birdie told me."

"I'll bet the alleged birdie is speaking through some cables, your screen, and a keyboard." Kingston blew out a long breath. "I suppose it would be in vain to tell you to mind ya business. Please don't go digging into what doesn't concern you, as it pertains to The Castle. I've met some of the Kings. These men would make formidable adversaries."

"Got it. I'll keep my end of the bargain because you asked. Just don't forget to bring me some more beer and …"

"Chinese food," they said at the same time.

Kingston's laughter died as he walked inside the foyer and stepped into the elevator that would take him to Ted's suite. When he walked out and approached the guard, the man met his gaze as if assessing him from the outside and moving inward to his soul. Kingston tipped his head but the dark-haired giant didn't return the gesture. He was obviously a professional not to be played with.

"My name is Kingston Coburn. I'm with Samantha DaCosta."

After pulling out his phone and looking at the screen, he nodded and stepped aside.

Kingston tapped the door and felt himself relax when Sam pulled it open.

She let him inside, then her gaze shifted over his shoulder. "Where's Ted? He said he was stepping out to have a word with you."

Frowning, Kingston said, "The last I saw him, Ted told me he was coming upstairs with you."

Sam gasped, then lifted Kingston's wrist to see the time. "I don't believe this. He's supposed to meet Daron and his team downstairs in a half-hour."

A picture flashed in his mind and Kingston closed his eyes. "You need to check with security."

"Why?" Sam turned the same kind of look on him that he'd just received from the guard. "Is there something you're not telling me?"

"It started raining hard, and I can't be certain, but I thought I saw an Audi like his going down the driveway five minutes ago."

Sam's mouth opened and she blinked as if he'd said the unthinkable. "Why on earth would he leave the premises when he knows the plan?"

Kingston thought he knew the answer but wasn't about to say anything to upset Sam or cause her to panic.

Chapter 10

Sam's eyes were dark pools of desperation when she pulled the phone from her ear. "He's not answering."

Kingston didn't miss the edge of fright in her voice, and squeezed her hand to provide comfort. "Give it another minute and try again. While you do that, I'll update security."

"He always answers my calls," she said, stopping in mid-stride.

Sitting next to her on the sofa, he kissed her forehead. "Don't assume the worst. Let's get the Kings involved."

She nodded, but the anxiety didn't recede from her eyes.

"Let me talk to this security guy and come right back, okay?"

She exhaled, then hit the speed dial button again.

Kingston unlocked the door with the security code Sam gave him. The moment it opened, the man faced him, poised for action.

"Ted DaCosta seems to be missing."

Aside from the shadows in his eyes shifting, the tall man only reached for his phone. He stepped away and spoke into it before returning to where Kingston stood. "Someone will be up in a few minutes. The two of you are to stay where you are now."

Kingston didn't like his tone, but now wasn't the time to let his ego rule him. Locating Sam's uncle was a priority, plus keeping her safe based on the threats made against her. For a moment, he wished Sam hadn't taken on the assignment that brought on all of this cloak-and-dagger maneuvering, but that was futile since her uncle would have had these issues whether or not she was writing a story.

He returned to sit next to Sam and gently extracted the phone from her hand. "He'll see that you called. I'm sure the Kings will have some ideas coming out of the meeting."

"I'm not one to give in to negativity, but I don't know what I'd do if something happens to Ted." Sam scooted closer and rested her head against his chest.

With one arm around her, Kingston slid his palm up and down Sam's arm. "He'll be fine. He hasn't lived this long without learning a thing or two about taking care of himself."

His words conveyed one thing, but Kingston was thinking another. Ted's move was reckless, but he hoped Daron and his team would find him before he got himself in some serious trouble.

After a heavy sigh, Sam spoke in a monotone. "My uncle is more supportive than my father. He doesn't judge me and were it not for him, you and I would never have met."

"I understand that."

"He gave me a safe haven when I first came here and supported me in every move I've made. When Father wanted me to become a doctor, Ted stood up to him and told him what I wanted. Don't try to live out your failings vicariously through Sam. That's what he told him." She tipped her head back, then continued, "That's when I knew my father started med school, but didn't make it through the first year. He tried that with my sister, but she set him straight right away."

Kingston hadn't heard Elias's story before, but realized Sam needed to talk through her issues and distract herself. He wanted to pull her into his lap and soothe her fears, but in a few minutes they would have company. Instead, he covered her lips with his, then murmured. "As long as I can help, I'll do everything to get us over this hurdle."

Eyes closed, she said, "In case I never told you before, I love you."

The time wasn't ideal for this kind of disclosure, which he suspected was why Sam was telling him now. She didn't want to explain her feelings or give him the opportunity to move them to what would be the next natural step. Head tipped to one side, Kingston did some mental hopscotch. The things he wanted to say to her would keep. Now, it was important to let her know he was in for the journey. "I love you too, babe."

The doorbell rang and Sam jerked in his arms.

"Stay here, hon. I'll get it."

He went to the door and held it open.

Carrying a fedora and a small oblong box, Daron walked into the room, followed by Shaz, Jai, another man who resembled him, plus a muscular, blond man, who hadn't been at the meeting.

"This is Nicco," Daron said, "He's part of my team and will be helping us with the negotiations."

"Please sit." Sam waved toward the expensive leather sofas positioned around the living room.

"We've confirmed that your uncle did leave the property," Daron said, spinning the hat he still held in his hands. "Do you have any idea why?"

Sam hunched with her arms across her stomach. "None at all. He was going to have a word with Kingston. At least, that's what he said, but he told Kingston he was coming back here."

The fourth man cleared his throat. "I'm Vikkas Germaine. We're told you saw him leaving. Do you know why he would have done that with such a limited time to meet the people making these demands?"

Kingston shook his head, but the man's gaze didn't waver.

"Let me put it this way," Daron asked, "Do you suspect why he might have left and where he was headed?"

Kingston considered what he knew and was at liberty to say. He reached for Sam's hand, stroking her silky skin as he said, "He might be trying to handle the situation on his own."

Daron pulled in a sharp breath and his gaze shifted to Nicco, who left the room. "I hoped you wouldn't say that."

Chapter 11

"I can't believe you knew that and didn't say anything." Sam cut her eyes at Kingston and yanked her hand out of his, despite his attempt to hold on to it.

"There's a difference between *knowing* and *suspecting*, Sam."

Arms folded, she spat, "You still could have said something."

"I could have, but I didn't want you to worry."

"And that's the standard answer a man gives a woman when he thinks she can't handle the truth." Sam raised her eyes to the ceiling before her focus went to the other men in the room, whose facial expressions hinted that they agreed with Kingston's approach. They didn't speak, but when they looked at him, their gazes conveyed commiseration.

"So, what's the plan?" she asked Daron, then let her attention shift to Jai, Nicco, then Shaz, and Vikkas.

Kingston dropped one hand on top of hers and squeezed, as if to caution her. But she was past the point of caring if these Kings thought she was pushy. The man she rated most, next to the one who had her heart, might be in mortal danger. His safety was all that mattered now.

"My guess would be that Kingston is correct." Daron dropped his hat on the coffee table and met her gaze.

"Why d'you think that?" Sam asked, her eyes fixed on him.

"There may be something your uncle doesn't want us to know, or he may have been threatened in such a way that he believed it was best to handle the situation under his own steam. Speaking of which, we brought a security measure for you."

He opened the oblong box and revealed a watch. When she stared at it, Daron said, "Aside from being a time piece, this device carries an electronic charge—"

"You mean like a stun gun?"

"Something very much like that." His smile disappeared when he continued, "If you're in danger, depressing the stem for a couple of seconds will activate it. Make contact and you can drop a fully-grown man."

"I don't know that I'll ever need this, but thank you." Cupping her face with both hands, Sam let out her breath. "Ted had help, what would make him think he needed to face these people alone?"

"It's probably a man thing. Ted would want to handle his business on his own. Especially if ..."

His words trailed off and Sam bet she wouldn't want to hear whatever platitude he had on the tip of his tongue.

"I won't tell you not to worry," Daron said, "but we've dispatched a team to track down your uncle and neutralize the situation, as necessary."

Shaz made a comment to Daron that she didn't hear and when Jai tapped his watch, she rubbed her temples and sat back. Every ounce of energy had drained out of her along with her spirit. When Kingston dropped an arm around her shoulder, Sam looked him dead in the eyes. "Are you thinking what I'm thinking?"

"That depends."

She smiled, but it didn't go past her lips. "We've never lied to each other," she murmured, "you don't need to start now."

Sam felt his deep intake of breath against her hair and understood he was still thinking of how to spin his words to bring her some kind of comfort. "What are you thinking, love?"

"That Ted is really trying to head something off at the pass, or he's trying to protect me."

With a slow nod, Kingston said, "That's what I'm thinking, too."

Sitting forward, she asked, "When will we know anything?"

"In a few more minutes." Daron shifted his attention to the phone in his hand at the sound of a muted ping. "Matter of fact, we have an update."

He read the screen, then turned his attention to Sam. "He's headed into a nightclub downtown. Do you have any idea what could be so important, he'd risk being someplace else other than where he's supposed to be?"

"That's out of character for him. Ted doesn't frequent those places even at night, so I don't know how to explain that." She edged sideways until her knees bumped Kingston's. "What's really going on here?"

***

Kingston wished he knew what to say to reassure Sam. Since he didn't, he remained silent. His phone buzzed and he got it out of his pocket. A text notification from Trey-Jon flashed on the screen.

Your guy might have known what was up with the MiVaxx products. That's why he's a target.

If Ted's dodgy behavior wasn't a clue, Kingston didn't know what was. When he raised his head, Daron and Shaz were watching him. Sliding a glance at Sam, he hoped he wasn't as transparent as these men made him feel.

Then he had an idea. He smiled, as if amused by what was on his phone screen, then typed a message to Daron, who was still looking at his phone. Kingston gave thanks for having the wisdom to take their contact information at the meeting.

To his credit, Daron didn't give a hint that anything was amiss. Directing a comment at Vikkas, he stood. "We should all be on location when Ted gets his instructions. Nicco and Angela, my security team members, will shadow him until we arrive."

Sam gave Kingston a hopeful look, which he met with a restraining one of his own. "One member of your family in danger is enough. Your father would kill me if anything happened to you."

"I didn't say anything," she protested, then grimaced.

"But I knew what you were thinking."

She tipped her chin higher. "You're not responsible for me."

Kingston studied Sam, who stared back in defiance. "Do you think Ted will care about that?" he asked.

She sighed and pushed one hand through her hair. "You're right. I'll stay put."

"As if."

As the men got to their feet, she asked, "What exactly does that mean?"

Leaning in close, Kingston spoke so that only the two of them heard his words. "No matter what I have to do, you will not be leaving this suite until we locate your uncle."

Through her teeth, she said, "Do I need to remind you that I can take care of myself?"

When Kingston sat back, the men were ready to leave.

Shaz dipped his head toward Sam. "Try not to worry too much. Daron is the best. Dro's also working on this. Your uncle will be fine."

She returned his gesture, then said, "Thank you."

His smile widened. "You remind me of my wife. You're both capable and independent." His attention went to Kingston and he added, "But like I tell her, sometimes it's good to listen to your king."

Sam's nostrils flared as if Shaz's advice and the play on Kingston's name irritated her. She lowered her gaze and clasped both hands. "Just bring my uncle back alive and in one piece."

Chapter 12

Kingston couldn't stand to see the tears glittering in Sam's eyes. Every so often, she delicately pressed a tissue to her face. Despite her questions, Ted hadn't done more than gloss over his willful disappearance and subsequent return. His pale-yellow shirt was grimy in the chest area as if he'd been lying on concrete, and he had faint bruises to one side of his face.

Nothing he said brought Sam any clarity, and Kingston suspected she wouldn't be getting any this evening. Ted left them under the guise that he'd gone into the shower, but he had more going on. He would likely use the time to come up with a story he thought would satisfy his niece.

When Ted walked back into the room, Kingston laid aside his iPad. He'd been scrolling through news items after Sam stopped speaking to him. He had tried telling her that approaching Ted with patience would work better than knocking him over the head with a mallet. But she wanted answers and didn't see the point in dancing around Ted's disappearance.

Sam focused on Ted, who stared at Kingston. The trace of hostility gave him the excuse he needed to leave. The tension had shot up by several degrees and making himself scarce would allow them to say things they couldn't with him present, so he stood. "I'm going outside for a bit to stretch my legs."

Neither of them answered, so Kingston slipped his phone into his jeans and left the suite. When he stood inside the elevator, the cellular buzzed. The message was from Daron.

Please meet us in the conference room downstairs. You have security clearance.

Before the team returned to the property, Kingston had received a text asking that he be present at a meeting. He didn't have to work his brain too hard to figure out why he was needed.

Within seven minutes, he arrived at the state-of-the-art conference room having passed through several security guards with no issues.

He stepped into the circular room, impressed once again by the tasteful yet obviously expensive furniture, the massive screen housed at one end, and the half-moon conference table that allowed the men to view each other without having to crane their necks.

Vikkas, who closely resembled Jai, invited Kingston to sit. Daron, Dro, Jai, Shaz, and another man, who was introduced as Hassan Khan were already seated. The glasses and saucers at their elbows told Kingston they had been there at least long enough to dull their appetites. When his stomach growled, Kingston remembered that he hadn't eaten anything other than the cocktail patties earlier in the afternoon. The situation hadn't left them any time to think about filling their bellies.

"Grab a plate and help yourself," Shaz said. "You're probably in the same situation as we are and haven't eaten anything since we were here hours ago."

"That's true." Kingston went to the credenza, a little guilty because Sam also hadn't eaten. Not because there wasn't food in the suite, but she wouldn't hear of it while they didn't know what had happened to Ted.

When he sat with a selection of delicate sandwiches with whisper-thin slices of chicken and roast beef and a glass of orange juice, Daron asked, "Where did you get the information you sent me?"

"I'm a reporter from the old school. I never reveal my sources."

Vikkas smiled and glanced down at the file on the table. "Your résumé implies you're a whole lot more than a simple reporter."

Dipping his head in acknowledgment, Kingston said, "Well, I've been known to break a story or two."

"Big ones, from what we've seen." Shaz bit into a sandwich, then added after a moment. "That alone negates the old-school reporter story you're trying to feed us. We need to know how much information your sources have on this matter. It's critical that we know what we're dealing with."

"Let's just say, some of the data I can access would mean me being in a spot if I were caught by the wrong people. The job gives something of an edge that way."

Dro's lips curved at the corners, but he didn't speak.

"Let me ask you this." Shaz wiped his mouth with a napkin. "Do *you* believe Ted knew what he was getting into when he invested in MiVaxx?"

Kingston had already asked himself the question a thousand different ways and still didn't have a conclusive answer. "I'm not sure about that one way or another. From what I've seen and heard, he certainly knows how to bluff."

"And this man he went to see, Bronson Hardy, what about him? What's your gut feeling?"

"Ted couldn't have chosen worse company."

"Why were you so sure that's where we would find him," Jai asked, making a steeple of his fingers under his chin.

Kingston considered how to word his answer as he wiped his fingers and dropped the linen napkin on the table's brilliant surface. "If I were in that kind of trouble, I'd look for help from someone who I thought could deal with the thugs on my back. Out of all his associates, Hardy fits that bill. They've been friends for a long time."

Jai nodded slowly and shifted to look at Daron, who said, "The man is into some things that isn't for the faint of heart."

Hassan spoke for the first time. "We need you to help us, so we don't have to waste manpower digging around when you have the details we need."

"What exactly do you want to know?" Kingston raised both eyebrows as he asked, "And how do you know I have that info?"

"Well," Shaz said, "We believe we're in proximity to the mother lode because we hit the principal vein based on the message you sent Daron."

"If you don't mind, can you tell me what happened inside that nightclub?"

"You're asking because …" Vikkas tipped one brow.

"Ted looked like he'd been run over when he came back." Kingston studied the faces around him. "We all know he didn't go out in that state."

Daron and Vikkas exchanged a glance, then focused on Kingston. After a nod Kingston almost missed, Daron swiped his phone screen. In a concise update, which Kingston suspected only covered the highlights, Daron told him that they arrived in time to prevent Ted from being kidnapped.

The owner of the nightclub hadn't been as lucky.

Chapter 13

"If I live to be a hundred, I'll never understand you men." Sam paced the living room, while Ted settled on one of the sofas.

Ted rubbed both sides of his forehead as he spoke. "You're going to make me dizzy if you don't stop wearing holes in the carpet."

"I can't help it." She glared at him. "What else can I do with all of this pent-up energy? I still don't know what you were thinking."

"It didn't seem like a good idea for me to sit around and wait while a set of thugs gave me instructions." His answer hinted at defiance but he avoided her gaze like a child unable to face his parents after lying about wrongdoing.

"So, instead you run into a situation where you're almost killed?"

"Nobody was trying to murder me." Ted's head shot up but again he didn't meet her eyes, which made her wonder what exactly took place earlier. A muscle-bound blond man and a dark-haired female had escorted him into the apartment and scanned the suite without appearing to do so. Had she not figured out that they were security, she might not have noticed that slick move.

Ted might think she was overreacting, but relief almost sent her into meltdown mode. That, and Kingston's stunt that she'd only discovered by accident.

When she and Ted had arrived at a stalemate, he went to the kitchen for a drink he didn't need. While he was there, she picked up Kingston's iPad that he'd left on the coffee table. She plugged in his PIN and found his email open. She minimized the screen, then scanned the open document underneath before she realized what she was reading.

The report, which concerned a specific individual, mentioned "the subject" several times, which made her uneasy. When her gaze went to the name of the document, she almost choked on her inhalation. Ted's name wasn't spelled out, but his three initials, plus his date of birth weren't hard to decipher.

Holding her breath, she read the file, skimming and stumbling in places. Her uncle was involved in more than he cared to admit. Her thoughts took off at a gallop and she didn't know whose neck she wanted to wring more—Ted or Kingston's.

What he'd done was an invasion of privacy, but she should have known that since he had ways and means, he would do what came naturally for a journalist. Was he writing his own story? She'd been naïve to think he wouldn't dig deeper if he was supposed to be helping her get information for her article. If he intended to share this information with her, she could excuse him. But, he hadn't said a word about this new data. And that made her believe he had another angle and agenda.

Her attention shifted to Ted, who looked away from her, suddenly fascinated by a watercolor painting of a woman balancing a basket on her head. A moment passed before he cleared his throat. "I'm sorry you were worried, but everything will be fine."

She didn't bother to tell him that his hangdog expression and the way he was slumped in the seat told a different story. The Perrier Carbonated Mineral Water still sat at his elbow and hadn't been touched. For the first time in ages, she didn't know what to say to him.

Kingston was a concern, too. That article he might be penning could make her work obsolete. He had all the right connections and expertise to write a compelling exposé. What the heck was he thinking?

She skimmed the report on Ted one more time, to memorize the content. Then she pulled up Kingston's email and put the screen to sleep. This was one time she wished he hadn't given her access to his iPad, but that was the nature of their relationship. They didn't hide the details of their lives from each other and since neither believed in searching for information that didn't concern them—except in their journalism—that agreement had worked well.

Until now.

"So what's next?" she asked, tucking away her angst over Kingston's possible betrayal to deal with at a later time.

Ted jerked in the seat and dragged one hand down his face. The bags under his eyes had developed within a few hours. She corrected herself. He'd been looking this way since she came to visit.

"The security will stay in place and I'll be extra careful." Ted's fingers drummed against the chair arm while he rubbed his forehead with his other hand. When Ted realized she was watching, he sat still.

The doorbell rang, which nearly catapulted him out of the chair.

Sam bit her lip to swallow laughter that was ill-timed, but her uncle made a funny picture as his limbs flailed in different directions. He settled back in the seat, but couldn't seem to keep his hand off his face. This time, he fingered the bruise that had darkened to a crimson hue. The sight of it annoyed her instead of rousing sympathy. The stubborn cuss still hadn't told her how he'd been injured.

She crossed the living room and answered the door.

Kingston stood in the carpeted passage, laden with at least a half-dozen bags. A glance at the colorful plastic told her he'd been to a Jamaican restaurant. Her smile blossomed until she remembered what he'd done, which caused it to disappear faster than a stick of butter on a hot griddle. She stepped aside and gave him room to enter.

He didn't move but tilted his head and one thick brow rose in a questioning manner. "Is everything okay?"

"As well as they can be under the circumstances, I suppose."

He touched his lips to her cheek and she inhaled deeply, her usual reaction when she'd been away from him for any length of time. He embodied everything she needed in a man. Affection. Passion. Strength. Kingston always felt like home. Even when he'd done something under-handed like that move she discovered this evening.

"How is Ted?" he asked as his attention went beyond her to the living area.

Instead of answering, she relieved him of several bags and opened one that contained a foil package. "I smell fried breadfruit. Did you go back to that place where we had lunch the other day?"

"No. Shaz introduced me to …" Kingston stopped, as if he'd said too much.

Already suspicious from her earlier discovery, Sam pounced. "And where exactly did you see him?"

"On the premises."

She peered into his eyes, certain he wasn't sharing all he knew. Kingston could be close-mouthed when he wanted to be, especially if it pertained to sensitive information. She wouldn't get anything more out of him right now, so she led the way to the kitchen.

He excused himself to wash his hands. By the time he returned, she had laid all the containers on the marble countertop. He asked no questions but leaned against the refrigerator while she opened drawers and cupboards and gathered the plates and cutlery they needed. She felt his gaze and sensed his curiosity, but didn't break the silence.

Let him stew because we both know he's keeping secrets. She also knew if he touched her again, almost everything would be forgiven. He would never relinquish that mysterious power he held over her body and senses—nor would she want him to.

He straightened and moved toward her and she swore he was about to ask what was wrong, but he only removed a serving spoon from her hand and murmured, "Let me help. You set the table."

"Fine."

In minutes, she laid out all the cutlery and although Ted wouldn't be in the mood to eat, she prepared a plate of fried breadfruit and a small serving of ackee and saltfish for him.

While Kingston served the food, she went to fetch Ted, who was scrolling through his phone.

"Did you get another message?"

He shook his head and mustered a weak smile. "I'm looking at my calendar."

She didn't believe him, but wouldn't force any issues. Sam had had enough of her uncle, her man, and their secrets.

"I've prepared a little something for you." She raised both hands when he protested. "No is *not* an option. You have to eat something."

When he rubbed his jaw, she said, "Do it for me. We can't afford for you to be sick."

He pushed himself to stand. "Fine. But I'm going to rest as soon as we're finished eating."

His weak excuse was another evasion she didn't acknowledge.

On impulse, when they sat at the table, Sam gripped each man's hand. Eyes closed, she said a heartfelt prayer of thanks for the meal they were about to have and the safety of the people in her life.

"Thanks, love." Ted's smile was strained but his eyes conveyed affection.

She patted his hand. "Please eat something."

He smiled again, and to her surprise tears burned her eyes. While she picked up the cutlery, Sam blinked to clear her vision. Ted meant so much more to her than she thought about at a conscious level. Though they were uncle and niece, they were very much alike in many ways— stubborn and persistent with whatever challenge faced them, plus fierce-ly loyal.

She felt fortunate to have him as the father figure in her life when Elias didn't have a clue how to let Sam be her own person and make the decisions she thought were best for her personal path. Ted allowed her the freedom to choose her areas of specialization and didn't police her friendships. She couldn't imagine life without him.

"I think it would be best if Sam stayed with you for a few more days while I fly to New York."

Kingston's words brought her back to the dinner table and the peppered steak that was halfway to her lips. "Um, I do have a say in *my* plans for the next week, Mr. Coburn."

He covered her wrist with one hand, and without warning his warmth aroused her and she shuddered. Her thighs relaxed as she remembered how long it had been since …

"I'm not trying to make decisions for you." He raised his thumb and index finger and held them a half inch apart. "But when Ted comes this close to being kidnapped, it makes sense for you to—"

She jerked her hand away at the interruption of her remembered pleasure and shifted her gaze between both men. "I'm sure you didn't just say what I heard."

Kingston's eyes flashed and he snarled at Ted, "You didn't tell her?"

Chapter 14

"Are you going to tell me what's really going on here?" Kingston stood with his back to the apartment door. Both hands rested in the pockets of his shorts to prevent him from flexing them. That's how restless he was, plus a low-level irritation rode him and he didn't want to lose his temper.

Sam's nostrils flared, then she tipped her head to one side and folded her arms. "You're the one who owes me an explanation."

"Maybe if you were more specific—"

"Don't play mind games with me, Kingston, when we've always been honest with each other."

Rubbing his forehead with one hand, he snapped, "For heaven's sake, just tell me what's on your mind. You've been here now for ten minutes and I still don't know why you're upset."

Sam's lips puckered in a gesture that reminded him of his mother's expression when she was displeased. "Fine. I picked up your iPad yesterday. You left a document open on the screen."

The queasy sensation in his stomach joined the mass in the region of his throat. He knew exactly which document he'd left open and accepted that the worst thing he could do was pretend like it didn't pertain to Ted, or that he hadn't ventured further than he should have. Sam was no fool and he wouldn't insult her intelligence by playing dumb.

"In case you forgot." She poked his chest. "Which I know you haven't. It's about my uncle."

"Oh."

She stood akimbo and cocked her hip. "That's all you're going to say?"

"I have no excuse." He brushed past her—working his brain to get out of the hole he'd dug for himself—knowing she'd follow him. "And I'm not about to make one up."

"You didn't need to invade his privacy."

"Says you." Facing her in the middle of the living room, Kingston continued, "Whatever he's doing has put you in danger. *That* gave me the right."

What he didn't say was that although Sam had security at The Castle, he still worried. Each time he woke during the night, Kingston's mind flashed to Sam and he asked himself what he would do if anyone hurt her.

She ran one hand through her hair, ruffling it. "And you didn't think about sharing the information with me?"

"Of course, I did, but I didn't want to give you anything more to worry over. You're under enough stress already." Seconds after studying her tired eyes, he murmured, "Come here."

She stared at him, still defiant as she scanned his body from waist to mid-thigh. "Let's be clear on this. I'm not giving in because you asked, but because you have what I need." Her eyes returned to the gentle bulge in his shorts. The battle between what she wanted and needed raged on.

After pulling Sam to his chest, Kingston spoke into her ear. "You are something else, but you know that. You're cussing me out but we're on pause now because you want … what exactly?"

She tipped her head back to meet his gaze. "You're not forgiven, but I need a hug."

While she nestled against his chest, Kingston stroked her hair and breathed in her perfume. The familiar combination of floral notes, vanilla, and light musk was refreshing, yet comforting. Sam was his place of rest and he never wanted that to change. The thought of her being in danger made him squeeze her tighter and dust her forehead with light kisses. His arousal from a moment ago dissipated into concern for her well-being and had to be set aside for another time.

"Everything will work out, babe. Nothing will happen to Ted. The Kings have him covered."

"You know," Sam murmured as if speaking to herself. "Maybe it would be a good thing for him to get out of the city."

Nodding, he said, "That's a smart plan. He's secure inside the walls of The Castle, but he must feel like a prisoner and a target if he knows someone is out there looking for him."

"I'll suggest it to him. It's been a while since he went home." She bit one corner of her lip while her eyes took on a faraway cast. "My father doesn't exactly get along with him, but Ted has several properties there, so that won't be an issue."

Stroking her back, Kingston asked, "How hard will it be to convince him?"

She thought about his words for a moment. "I suppose it would be easier if I said I'd go with him. That way, he wouldn't have to worry about me."

Kingston inched backward and asked, "Aren't you setting yourself up for more issues if you go back to Jamaica and don't visit your people?"

Eyes flashing, Sam clenched her jaw. "I'm sure you heard my father say that if I left the way I did, I shouldn't come back."

He didn't try to placate her. Sam knew her father's disposition and when the time would be right to approach him. "What about work?" he asked. "Didn't you plan to be back in the office in another week or so?"

She nodded, thinking they'd lived through such a long period of wearing masks and constant hand sanitizing that it was almost weird to be out and about without face coverings. "This pandemic has taught all of us that we can work from just about any place we choose. Catherine is still working remotely most of the time. I'm sure I can convince her to allow me to work from Jamaica. As long as I stay on track with my stories, she'll be fine."

"This plan is sounding better by the minute." He gripped Sam by both arms and searched her eyes. "About the information on your uncle, I'm sorry, but I had to do it. I needed to know what I was dealing with."

She arched one brow. "And? Why do I have the feeling your scheming tech guru, Trey-Jon is in on it, but not me?"

"You know where I stand when it comes to information and my sources. You don't want to talk about Evita but you wanna question me about Trey-Jon's involvement?"

Glaring, she asked, "Are you kidding me?"

"You know I'm not. Let's just say your uncle has invested his money in some interesting ways."

"So, what about the other folks,"—she gave him a sour look—"you know, the ones you were *supposed* to be researching for me?"

"Now *that*, I can help you with, but before we deal with that matter …" He drew her closer with an arm around her waist and breathed against her neck. When the tip of his tongue trailed across her skin, Sam gasped. He covered her mouth with his, and they exchanged a slow, arousing kiss that left Sam clinging to him. Talk about a sweet diversion.

A buzzing sound interrupted them, and Kingston frowned as he pressed another kiss to her lips. "What the heck is that?"

"My phone. It's on vibrate," she said. "Give me a minute."

They eased apart and she slid it out of the back pocket of her jeans. Curiosity filled her eyes as she put the cellular to her ear. "Mom, what's up?"

She listened without speaking for at least a minute, while Kingston observed how her lips trembled and the sharp intake of breath. He didn't interrupt, but when Sam gripped a handful of his tee-shirt in one fist, Kingston knew she'd received bad news. He led her to the sofa where they settled next to each other.

"Okay, I'll make the arrangements."

With extra care, Sam placed the phone on the coffee table, then slid her cold hand into his. The smudges under her eyes seemed to have darkened. She swallowed hard while rubbing her arms, causing the soft material of her blouse to bunch above her elbows. "My father had a heart attack."

Chapter 15

Life-threatening illness was unfortunate at any time, but in this case it served a useful purpose.

Sam accessed all the passes she needed with ease. Catherine had quickly acquiesced to time off, plus continued remote job functions. Ted hadn't hesitated to say yes to coming home. In fact, he'd seemed relieved at the thought of leaving Chicago, not that he admitted any such thing. But his air of expectancy and improved mood told a clear story.

After a conference call among Daron, Kingston, and Ted, the Kings arranged for a local security team to meet them at the airport and shadow them during their stay. Ted had no trouble with footing the bill. After all, he'd put himself in this position. Or so, Kingston seemed to think.

Ted had made their flight arrangements through his travel agent and three hours later, they were en route to the capital city that shared Kingston's name. All the test requirements due to the COVID-19 virus had been squared away, thanks to Ted and now he and Kingston sat in the waiting area of the University Hospital of the West Indies' private wing.

Visiting hours were almost over, but the head nurse on duty had given Sam the leeway to see her father after she explained the situation.

She tapped the door and opened it when her mother gave permission to enter. Sharon DaCosta sprang to her feet and wrapped her arms around Sam. "Thank God you're here."

Sam stifled alarm at the sight of her father's blotchy, pale complexion, over her mother's shoulder. His eyes were closed and his face was drawn.

"What happened," Sam asked, resting both hands on her mother's shoulders. "And where's Michele?"

"She was here earlier." Mom blinked hard, as if trying to stay awake. "She has a showing this evening."

"So what did the doctors say?"

"They put in a stent which will keep the blood flowing and stop his arteries from narrowing again."

Sam released her mother and sighed. "You have to encourage him to make more healthy food choices."

Glancing behind her, Sharon said, "Maybe this will make him take his health more seriously. I've been trying to convince him to walk with me in the mornings, but he's a stubborn man."

"I can hear you talking about me." His lashes fluttered, then his eyes opened. When her father's gaze landed on her, a smile touched his lips then vanished. "I thought I told you not to come back after your disgraceful behavior?"

Elias DaCosta hadn't lost his spunk or the desire to punish her for loving Kingston. Although he'd been rude, Sam used wisdom and tempered her response. "Despite the way you treated my guest, you're still my father."

"Well—"

"Father." She raised one hand, which silenced him. "I'm not doing this with you. How are you feeling?"

He squinted at her as if he couldn't decide whether or not to act outraged.

"I'm doing very well." He shifted, and a quickly disguised wince told Sam he was lying. "And I intend to live for many more years, no matter what the doctors say."

"That's good to know." She stood by the bedside and touched his hand. "I'm glad you're still here."

"If he'd slow down, his chances of staying above ground would be even better." Sharon eased into the chair next to him and shook her head.

"If I stop going to work, you may as well call the undertakers." Elias chuckled, but Sharon didn't join him. Nor did Sam.

His grin slid away and he asked, "How long are you here?"

"As long as I need to be," she said, giving him a defiant stare.

He sniffed, then asked, "Did you come alone?"

"Father—"

"Answer me."

"No, your *brother* came with me."

That wasn't what he wanted to hear and Elias tried to sit up. "You know exactly what I mean."

Sharon rose and pressed him back to the pillow. "You're going to undo the doctor's work. Mind your business and concentrate on getting better."

His narrow nostrils flared and he sucked his teeth. "I should have known all of you would come flocking around like vultures. John crows, all of you, waiting to see if I dropped dead."

Her father's words were like a slap to the face. Sam weighed hers before speaking. In a calm voice she said, "I don't know what has happened to you. Instead of thanking God you're still alive, you choose to throw insults that only make you look small and petulant."

Despite her cool delivery, Elias' face flushed. "He hasn't come around in years and now he feels the need to show up? He's the reason you've turned into a rebel."

"Father, please stop this—"

"See, this is what I mean. I used to be your Papa, and nowadays–"

"Okay, *Papa*. Don't, please." Sam gripped his thick wrist and squeezed. "I didn't come here to fight you. Since my presence upsets you so much, I'll leave. Do you want to see your brother or not?"

"I think I'll pass on that pleasure this evening," he said, twisting out of her grip.

With a sigh, Sam stepped back. "Mom, a word please."

Risking more rejection, Sam bent over her father and kissed his forehead. "I love you."

Elias stared straight ahead as if he were alone in the room. His reaction cut Sam to the core, but aside from pulling in a sharp breath she didn't react.

After throwing a glare at him, Sharon followed Sam into the corridor. "Will I see you at home?"

Sam hugged her mother and kissed her cheek. "No, I'll stay with Ted. We both know Papa was serious when he said not to come back. And I haven't forgotten how both of you treated Kingston."

Sharon lowered her gaze. "You know why I reacted that way."

"Actually, I don't," Sam shot back. "But there's no need for an explanation now. This isn't the time. Come and say hello to Ted, then we can leave. What time do visiting hours start in the morning?"

"Ten o'clock," Sharon said, walking abreast of Sam. "He won't be in a better mood," she warned.

"Doesn't matter. Those who know better do better."

They turned the corner, which opened into the elegant waiting area. The two men who met them at the airport stood at the entrance.

Sharon barely glanced at them before walking past.

Kingston was flipping through a magazine, while Ted stared across the room. Both men stood when the women stopped inches from them.

Ted's attention went from Sam to her mother and back. Then he gave Sharon a warm smile and pulled her into a hug. "It's good to see you."

Her skin was flushed when she stepped away and slid a glance at Sam. "Likewise."

At the sight of Kingston, she forced a smile. "Hello."

"Good evening, ma'am. I'm sorry to hear about your husband."

"Thankfully, he will be well." She bared her teeth in another false smile, then clasped her hands. "I have to get back to the room."

"Can I see Elias for a moment?" Ted asked.

"I don't think that's a good idea right now." Sharon hurried away, leaving Ted frowning.

"What's going on?" he asked, sitting adjacent to Kingston.

Sam perched on the couch that looked as if it belonged in someone's living room as she rubbed the spot between her eyes. "Papa is being his usual disagreeable self."

"Even on a hospital bed, he has time to act like a fool?" Ted asked, his tone hinting at impatience.

"You know Papa better than any of us." Massaging her temples, she added. "It's best if we come back in the morning."

"Sure." He exchanged a glance with Kingston, then cleared his throat. "We've had an update on the situation with my friend Bronson."

"What's that?" She reached for Kingston's hand.

"The Kings tracked him to where he was being held." Ted shifted and sat closer to the edge of his seat. "They got him back …"

Her stomach bunched as she said, "But?"

"They're sure this isn't over. Although they captured the men who did the kidnapping, the mastermind behind it is still at large." He inhaled deeply, the lines etched deeper in his forehead.

Gripping Kingston's hand tightly, she said, "There's still more, right?"

"They're releasing that article about the vaccine tomorrow morning." Ted dragged his knuckles across his eyes. "And they haven't given up on finding me."

"And why exactly would they still be looking for you after all of this?" Sam asked, her voice laced with suspicion.

Ted shook his head. "Who knows how these people think?"

"What does this mean?" she asked Kingston.

"A new level of security." He glanced in Ted's direction. "Ted and I feel it would be better to head to the country tomorrow, after the Kings' security expert flies in tonight."

"So we're going into hiding?" she spat, aggravated that the pieces of this puzzle were not fitting together to bring any kind of comfort or sense of safety.

"I wouldn't put it that way." Ted brushed at his pants in an obvious attempt to avoid interfacing with her.

"Then how exactly would you describe us having to be shunted from place to place?"

Kingston eased closer and dropped his arm around her shoulder. "Hon, don't think of it that way—"

"Don't tell me how to think." She leapt to her feet and glared at them, knowing she was about to take her father's foolishness out on the wrong people. Sam opened her mouth to blast them, but instead sucked her teeth as she headed for the exit. "Frankly, I'm fed up with you men."

"You can't leave us, Sam. That could be dangerous," Kingston said, rising from the seat.

She flipped the hair over her shoulder as she stalked through the door. "Try and stop me."

Chapter 16

Kingston approached the bed where his suitcase lay open. He'd removed the few items he needed because of their plans to drive to Ocho Rios. Ted's townhouse in St. Andrew was where they would crash for the night.

After leaving the hospital, they stopped at a Chinese restaurant and bought dinner. Sam had barely said two words during the ride and they shared little conversation as they filled their stomach with cashew chicken, curried beef, special fried rice, and stir-fried vegetables.

She entered the room behind him, wrapped both arms around his waist, and pressed her body along the length of his back. He stood straight and threw a tee-shirt on the bed, but she didn't release him. Knowing she needed time to process whatever she was feeling, Kingston caressed her hands, which were clasped tightly on his belly.

"I'm sorry," she said, her voice low against the hum of the air conditioner. "I had a moment back there."

"I understand better than you think." When he tried to change his position, Sam wouldn't allow him to move. He continued speaking and stroking her skin. "I just wish you'd talk to me instead of getting into a temper. It's not safe for you to stalk away as if our lives are the same as usual. I don't need to remind you how things have changed in just a few short days."

She breathed against his tee-shirt. "I wish I hadn't started that stupid investigation."

Smiling, Kingston said, "If I recall correctly, you've said that to me before. So, I'll tell you again. Even if you did nothing, you couldn't change anything. And while I'm at it, let me remind you that watch doesn't make you superwoman."

When she didn't speak, but pressed her face to the muscles in his back, he asked, "Are you going to release me so I can hug and kiss my woman?"

That made Sam laugh and loosen her grip enough for him to turn and pull her to his chest. After a tender squeeze, he sat and pulled her down to sit across his lap.

"We're in an uncomfortable place right now, but we'll get through this."

"Speaking of that." Sam's slender fingers teased his scalp as if to massage the truth out of him. "What exactly happened today?"

Staring at their reflection in the full-length mirror across the room, he said, "Everything that took place this morning feels like it was a lifetime ago."

Hugging his neck, she said, "It feels the same for me. As if I'm in a time-travel movie or something."

Kingston cracked a smile, but wasn't amused. He re-lived scenes from earlier today as they spooled through his mind. Chicago seemed like a lifetime ago, but here they were hours later in another country.

While they retrieved Ted, the Kings had firmly kept Kingston out of the way, sitting in an air-conditioned luxury van. He'd been restless when after five minutes, none of them returned. His gaze never wavered from the doorway of the building they had entered, so the sight of Nicco and Angela hustling Ted between them across the street told him something was wrong.

A black Ford Taurus squealed out of a side road near the building and sped away with an SUV in pursuit.

Kingston asked no questions—Ted's bruised and sweaty face stopped him—but he understood what unfolded, based on the other men's questions.

In a shaky voice, Ted explained, "A pair of thugs grabbed Hardy, who was across the room from me. They forced him out the back of the building while Nicco and the others were on their way in through the front."

"What happened to your face?" Angela asked.

Ted put a hand to his cheek and winced. "I'd rather not talk about that."

That's when Kingston realized that he didn't know how they had tracked Ted to Hardy's location to rescue him. Trey-Jon's skills came to mind, plus the Kings seemed capable of so much more.

Once he decided where to begin, Kingston told Sam what he knew of the operation. He ended by saying, "I don't want you worrying about a situation you can't change. The men helping your uncle are professionals. That's clear from the little I've seen, so there's no point wearing out your brain."

She was silent for several seconds before she sighed. "I don't like feeling as if I'm being hunted. That, and my father's craziness, has me unsettled."

"Let's do what we can and leave the rest to God and time, right?"

"I guess." A moment went by before she shifted on his lap. "And what will *you* be doing?"

He grinned. "If I were you, I wouldn't worry about that. I'll do what I do."

"Mmm-hmm," she said in a grudging tone. "Just don't let my family's business be part of what you're doing."

Laughing softly, he asked, "Are you going to beat me over the head with that?"

Sam glanced toward the open door as she said, "You bet."

While wrapping his arms around her waist, Kingston latched on to Sam's neck.

She thumped him lightly on the chest. "Don't. You'll leave a mark."

"Aren't you your own woman?" he whispered, still nibbling her skin until she stiffened as if suddenly out of sync with his usual playfulness and familiarity with her body.

"Yeah, but you know how it is. While we're here …"

He relaxed his hold. "I get it. We have to conform to your family's wishes and act as if we're not together."

Sam splayed both hands across his chest as she searched his eyes, then her nostrils flared. "If that was the case, we wouldn't be staying here with Ted."

"Right, but I suppose in the morning when we go back to the hospital, it will be the same thing all over again."

"Why are you making a big deal of this? It's not as if you don't know how my parents feel about us."

"That's correct." He stared across the room as if she'd disappeared. "I keep forgetting."

They both knew that was a lie. Since their last visit, several things remained unsaid about her parents' attitude. Nor had they discussed where their relationship was going. They'd been together long enough to know they loved each other and were meant to be together. At least, he believed that. Sam, it seemed, was more concerned about what her family thought about their racial difference.

"Don't come at me like that." She shimmied off his legs to stand akimbo. "It's not as if your people like me any better."

Rubbing his jaw, Kingston said, "Be honest with yourself, Sam. My parents aren't the major problem here. How they may feel about you doesn't affect us. Ask yourself why you get uneasy in our relationship every time you see or talk to your mother and father."

She swept the hair away from her face and narrowed her eyes. "You're being unfair."

Kingston supported his weight on both hands, which he spread behind him, as he studied Sam. "Am I?"

"You don't see me bringing up your mother's remarks about you finding a nice Chinese girl to marry."

"Nor do I bring up …" He stopped himself by dragging both hands down his face. "Why are we doing this?"

Her shoulders rose and fell on a deep breath, then she shrugged. "I don't know, but I don't like it."

Kingston stood and kissed her forehead. "Go to bed, Sam, and stop taxing your brain."

"I'll say it again." Sam's hazel eyes darkened and watered. "You're being unfair."

"In what way? I'm not the one who refuses to take the next step." Kingston bit his bottom lip, trying to stop the flow of his thoughts that he'd held inside for too long. He couldn't, so he released the words he should have spoken a while back. "Why do you think I still take the risks I do? If I knew you were committed to a future with me, I'd have a ring on your finger before you could blink. As for going to China—"

"You're still thinking about that? Really?" She backed up and narrowed her eyes. "Don't blame me for the fact that you're a coward."

"What?" Her rude words knocked him sideways.

"My parents aren't the reason we haven't … you know. If you were sure about us, you'd have set them straight from the get-go."

"I can't sort out the issues you're not willing to face."

She poked him in the chest. "I do *not* have issues."

Kingston stood and gently led her to the door. "I love you, Samantha, but I'm not arguing with you all night."

She remained inside the threshold, arms folded while she glared at him. "I'm not the one who started this."

"Agreed." Kingston kept his voice even as he said, "I take the blame. I shouldn't have mentioned what happened earlier."

Shaking her head, Sam said, "Sometimes, you make me mad enough to—"

Ted walked into the living room and Kingston's gaze shifted to him over Sam's shoulder.

Moving to one side, she looked at her uncle, then back at Kingston. "This isn't finished. Not by a long stretch."

She marched to the other side of the living room, entered one of the bedrooms along the passage, and closed the door.

In response to Ted's questioning gaze, Kingston said, "Lovers' tiff. We'll work it out."

Standing behind the closed door, he sighed. Although he was ready for bed and would have done better wrapped around Sam as they slept, out of respect for Ted, Kingston chose not to share the same bed with her. While he put in some time writing, he'd unravel his thoughts.

Tomorrow, they would be on the move early. Tonight, he'd finalize the details with the Kings to ensure they remained safe.

Chapter 17

"Nobody asked you to come here." Elias threw his brother a glare filled with pure hate. "In fact, it would have been better if you had pretended not to be on the island because I could have done without seeing you."

Shocked and disgusted, Sam cried, "Father! What is wrong with you?"

Elias turned glittering eyes on her. "You expect me to lie because he decided to stop in and see me? Last night, I told you and your mother I didn't want him around, but you didn't listen."

Ted rocked on the balls of his feet, then sighed. "You're a sad little man. You know that? After all these years, you haven't changed."

Cursing, Elias struggled into a sitting position, while Sharon tried pressing him back to the mattress. "Let go of me," he yelled.

"None of this is helping you. Please lie down," she pleaded.

"I. Will. Not." His chest heaved as he gave her a narrow-eyed stare. "*You* are the cause of this. I told you last night."

Ted spoke from across the room. "Now that I know this is how you feel, I'll leave."

"Good," Elias shouted, lunging sideways. "And don't come back!"

Sam stared at her father, dumbstruck. How could he behave this way with his brother, especially after going to death's door and back?

"Before I go, I have one question." Ted ran one hand over his hair while frowning. "What did I ever do to you?"

"You shouldn't have to ask." Elias cut his eyes from Ted to Sam.

"So, now we're playing word games?" Ted said, with a trace of amusement coloring his voice.

"You stole my daughter," Elias yelled. "Put all sorts of ideas in her head. If I'd known when we sent her to you that you'd wreck her—" Sam's attention went to Sharon when she trembled, but she dismissed that reaction as her imagination. Her focus went back to Elias as he continued his rant. "—I'd have made sure she went to university right here."

"You couldn't *make* me do anything." Sam stared into her father's eyes. "You might have paid the fees initially, but Grandma is the one who funded my education. She saw to it after you cut me off for not staying under your thumb and studying at the University of the West Indies."

"I had every right as a father to decide where you completed your studies."

Sam shook her head, but didn't answer. She had to be missing something because her father wasn't making much sense. He'd never been an overly affectionate man so the accusation thrown at Ted was nonsensical. Almost.

"Elias, please stop this." Sharon stepped between the two men. "Ted, I think you'd better go."

"Fine, but you …" He tipped his chin at Elias. "… should be ashamed of yourself. Petty and jealous over your own child. What kind of foolishness is this?"

With a trembling finger, Elias pointed at Ted. "You're the one who's given her these liberal ideas. Before you put this stupidity in her head, Sam would never have considered having a relationship with a … someone outside of her race and status."

"Are you listening to the bull you're spewing, Elias? This isn't the

1930s. You may wish to think we're pure-blooded but we're not. We are exactly what the Jamaican motto says, 'Out of many, *one people*.' Keep fooling yourself. Have a nice life."

"And the same to you," Elias spat.

Sam followed Ted to the door, only to have her father ask, "Where are you going?"

She turned to meet his gaze. "Yesterday, you reminded me that you didn't want to see me."

Massaging his chest, Elias choked out, "If you leave this room—"

"Save it, Father. Your threats don't mean much anymore. I've had enough." She shrugged. "And if you can't accept Kingston, what's the point of me hanging around?"

Her mother sank on the chair with a hand to her forehead. The gemstones in her bracelet glittered, reminding Sam that her mother was living a lie. Sharon might look as if she had all of life's material comforts, but her existence with Elias could be nothing other than miserable. Strange how Sam had never noticed her parents weren't in love with each other until she moved out of their house.

"Mom, I'll talk to you later." When her gaze strayed to Elias, his head swung the other way and he found a pointed interest in an abstract painting across the room.

In the corridor, Sam caught up with Ted who didn't speak but dropped one hand over her shoulder and walked her to where Kingston waited with their guards.

***

While shaking the security consultant's hand, Sam tipped her head back to study him. "You do resemble Shaz a bit."

"That would be because we're cousins." He chuckled and stepped back to let them inside the five-bedroom villa, where they would be staying for the next week. Dorian "Ryan" Bostwick had arrived on the island and made it there before them. So had the Vikkas-and-Jai lookalike, who had traveled from Chicago and would also be in residence.

"I'm Hassan Maharaj," he said, with a charming grin. "The Kings have loaned me to you for the next couple of weeks."

Kingston dropped the suitcases he carried and held out one hand. "And you're related to the twin lawyer-and-doctor duo."

"That's right. Ryan and I will be scoping out the property to make sure you are all secure."

Sam could have sworn a conspiratorial exchange passed between them, as if they had met before today.

"We appreciate your help," Ted said, as he wheeled his traveling case through the front door.

A tall, slender woman in a pink uniform walked into the open, marble-tiled space. She greeted Ted with a warm smile. "Mr. Ted, welcome. We been longing to see you."

The two embraced, and while it didn't surprise Sam, the men around them watched with varying degrees of shock etched on their faces.

Stepping back, Ted explained, "Everybody, meet Violet. Her mother works for the family, as well. She and Charles, plus the rest of the team, take care of my properties here on the North Coast.

At the mention of his name, an older man with graying hair, dressed in a white shirt, black pants, and matching vest appeared behind Violet. "Sorry, Mr. Ted, I was on de roof."

"No need to apologize. It's been a while, eh?"

The man wiped his forehead with a handkerchief. "Yeah, it look like yuh abandon us."

"Not at all, Charles. Just busy, that's all."

The two shook hands before exchanging a man hug and pounding each other on the back.

"How is Mr. Elias?" Charles asked, sliding the hanky into his pocket.

A shadow crossed Ted's face, then he shrugged. "He's in the hospital, but he'll be fine. My brother is as contrary as the wind. But when has that ever been different?"

The memory of her father's ungracious treatment of his brother made Sam's mood dip, but not for long.

At the sight of Sam, Charles' face split in a wide grin and he opened his arms.

Sam walked into his embrace and gave her uncle's combination butler and property manager a tight squeeze. The smell of his skin, which had been exposed to the sun, took her back to childhood. "Hi, Uncle Charles."

"Howdy, Likkle Miss."

She had many fond memories of the man who had allowed Michele and her to tag along while he did his chores. He'd always been patient with them, answering their non-stop questions and picking flowers for them while sharing interesting tidbits about each variety.

This was the way of things in Jamaica. Those employed as domestics often became part of the family that employed them.

The moment the introductions were over, Violet asked, "Would anybody like somet'ing to drink?"

Ted, Kingston, and Sam welcomed that offer, and soon, the men were spread around the living room discussing how the security arrangement would work, since their villa was one of ten on the lush property, deliberately landscaped to resemble the forest. Each house was afforded privacy by wooden fencing at the back and around the deck, as well as tall hedges. Although the community was gated, Ryan and Hassan insisted they would walk the premises to scout for possible entry and exit points.

A half-hour after Charles got one of the housemen to bring their luggage upstairs, they split up and Sam followed Kingston to the room he'd be occupying.

She went to the door and stepped onto the balcony. The kidney-shaped pool beckoned and Sam knew she'd be in the water before the day ended.

"Hey, Kingston, did you bring swimming trunks?"

"Yeah, why?"

A mischievous grin stole across her lips as delicious thoughts swept through her mind. "Want to have a swim later?"

His answer didn't come immediately and after scanning the white-sand beach and calm aquamarine water in the distance, she went back inside. He still hadn't said anything about what he was doing with the information he hadn't given her, but Sam knew he was writing. Late last night when she'd gone to the kitchen for a snack, his light was still on. He'd always said he did his best work after hours. The need to clear the air bothered her. Now would be the best time to lay her suspicions to rest. She hated feeling she couldn't trust him.

Kingston stood by the bathroom door looking at his phone. He frowned, then scrolled up the page and scratched the back of his head as if puzzled.

She was almost under his nose before he looked up with concern in his gaze.

"Is everything all right?"

While rubbing his jaw, he said, "Yeah, nothing to worry about. Work."

Sam raised one brow, then positioned herself in front of him and rested her bare feet on the front of his boots. "Are you sure? You looked as if you received some bad news."

"Trust me. All will be well." Kingston slipped both arms around her.

"Right. I know you're trying to distract me." She trailed one finger down his jawline. "Does it have to do with that article you're writing?"

Frowning, Kingston pulled his head back. "Which one?"

She met his gaze. "Don't act like you don't know what I'm talking about."

"I wish you wouldn't do this."

"What exactly?" She tipped her chin up, still searching his eyes.

"Blindside me with accusations. If you have something to say, why don't you spit it out?"

"Okay. Fine. It seems to me that you're putting together the same story—"

Kingston's phone vibrated against her hip, and he looked at the screen. A tic developed under his eye. When he raised his head, she asked, "Something wrong?"

He shook his head and reeled her in again. "Everything's cool."

The man was flat-out lying. Another reason for her to doubt him. Kingston's heart was beating faster than was warranted, given that he was standing in place. Instead of reassuring her, his words set her nerves jangling. He hadn't said there was no need to be alarmed, which would have been a normal response. If everything would be fine, what had made him react this way?

Chapter 18

"Have you been holding out on me again?"

Samantha's words pulled Kingston out of his mental dilemma. He didn't like the question, but from her light tone, Sam was in a better mood.

The square of well-kept grass in the backyard below, surrounded by showy allamanda blooms in deep pink, yellow, and rust, was idyllic. The pool beckoned, reminding Kingston of their dip last night where they had kissed and fondled each other, forgetting they were in full view of the upstairs bedrooms.

Biting his lip, Kingston stifled a grin. Sam was adventurous and slick, wrapping her arms and legs around him and using her toes in sneak attacks on his groin. All of this while she clung to his back. The memory had him shifting in his seat to find a comfortable position.

He reached across the glass-topped, wrought iron table and laced their fingers together.

Sam had come back to his room with him after a sumptuous breakfast. The escoveitched fish—fried snapper filet doused with julienned carrots and onions in a vinegar marinade—went down well with fried plantain, and bammies, a kind of cassava cake. Since then, they had both been silently working on their individual stories.

"No, I'm not hiding anything," he finally answered. "Matter of fact, I've been doing some research and reading news items off the wire."

He'd postponed his trip to China because he couldn't go until he was sure Sam and her uncle were out of danger. Thing was, he hadn't told her about the change in plans. She hadn't given him the chance the other night when they were arguing over next to nothing. Episodes like that threw him off balance and made him doubt their compatibility. He put those negative thoughts aside and focused on the present.

In all the drama between Elias and Ted, and them moving from the capital city to Ocho Rios, Sam had forgotten about the article the people threatening Ted had said they would release, but Kingston hadn't. He debated whether to hide the truth, but it wouldn't serve him well.

Only a matter of time stood between Sam and the articles splayed across the pages of the newspapers and gossip columns in the States. The only advantage now was that Ted was out of the country and didn't have to deal with the media shoving recording devices in his face the minute he appeared in public.

He handed Sam the iPad he'd been using. "You need to see this."

As she read the details about her uncle being part of a company that produced vaccines that were suspected to have caused sterilization, and other side effects, to unsuspecting people in African countries, the color drained from her face. She set the iPad down in the middle of the table, pushed back the chair, and stalked into the bedroom.

Kingston leapt from his chair and moved swiftly to shut the door when she opened it. He turned Sam to face him. "What, exactly, are you planning to do?"

"I'm going to ask him about it."

With one hand still on the door, Kingston said, "Ask or accuse?"

She met his gaze, exposing the creamy skin of her neck. When she sighed, her breath wafted across his skin.

"All you're going to do is make him defensive if you run up on him like a freight train that has jumped off the track."

She huffed and folded both arms in a defensive gesture. "If these things *are* true, you think he deserves anything else?"

"What he deserves is neither here nor there right now," he argued. "Your responsibility is to get the facts, or as much of it as he has."

While she considered his words, Kingston removed his weight from the door.

For a couple of seconds, Sam closed her eyes. When she opened them, they were dark and stormy. "This story … it doesn't gel with the man I know. Ted is kind and caring. Always defended me from my father when he behaved like a tyrant. How could he involve himself in something that would cause suffering and pain to anyone? I just don't get it."

"I don't either, but let's do the work. See what else we find. It may well be that he's involved in this for a reason you don't understand right now."

"Oh, God." She put both hands to her head. "I don't even want to think about the legal implications."

"Let's not buy more trouble, okay?" Kingston's mind had already run down that path hours ago, but he preferred dealing with facts and not venturing into future problems unnecessarily.

She released an audible breath and brushed past him to turn on the television. With the remote pointed at the screen, she sank on the bed flipping through the channels. At every news station, she stopped and waited for the item on MiVaxx to air.

Kingston didn't stop her. News was their business. She'd get her fill of the story from every angle, then deal with it in the best way she knew how. He only hoped she wouldn't say anything to damage the relationship with her uncle. She'd already struck out with her father. Alienating Ted wouldn't leave her in a good place. Having two of three important men in her life go emotionally and physically MIA might do her irreparable damage,

He went back to the patio, picked up his phone, and sent a message to Trey-Jon. *The story is out.*

As he watched, a line of dots appeared, then Trey-Jon's message came through. *Yeah. I saw that. I have some news for you about the kidnapping. Let's talk.*

Kingston glanced up to be certain Sam was where he left her. *Don't call me. I'll call you.*

Trey-Jon's response was quick. *Usually, I'd be offended by that, but I understand this time.* When he received Trey-Jon's thumbs up sign, Kingston rose from the table. He stepped inside the room and Sam met him half-way across the carpet. Her shaking hands and pale skin gave away her agitation.

"What's wrong?" Kingston asked.

She smoothed the hair that had escaped back into a loose ponytail. "Sometimes, I think Ted has a death wish."

"Why would you say that?"

Sam bumped into Kingston on her way around him and paced to the balcony and back.

His gaze followed her as he stepped out of her way. "Are you going to answer me?"

"Yes, sorry. I'm just … I don't even know what I am right now."

"I understand," Kingston said in an even tone although Sam's behavior disturbed him.

She shook her head, then the fire returned to her eyes. Two splotches of color blossomed and spread on her cheeks as she spat, "I'd give an arm and a leg to find out how the media knows Ted and I are in the Caribbean."

Chapter 19

Michele whistled, then said, "So about dat dramatic visit to di hospital—"

"Let's get something straight, I didn't bring any drama." Sam moved the phone from one ear to the other. "All of this is Papa's doing. The man is worse than normal. What happened since I left?"

"I know yuh don't want to hear dis." Her sister lowered her voice when she continued. "But he's been dis way since yuh walk out o' di house wid Caramel King."

"When is he getting out of the hospital?" Sam asked, ignoring Michele's quip as she stared at the still blue waters of the Caribbean Sea. The early morning air carried a chill, but in minutes the sun would emerge and dry the droplets that lingered on the leaves and blades of grass in the back garden.

"Should be today. Di nurses' will be glad to see di back of him."

"I can well imagine." She turned away, then spun at the sound of a muted splash below. Kingston had dove into the pool. His muscles rippled as he cut through the water with strong strokes. If she wasn't on the phone, she would have joined him in several heart beats—despite the low-level resentment she still harbored.

"Why yuh so secretive?" Michele asked, her voice intense. "Yuh couldn't tell me yuh was coming?"

Despite her mixed emotions, Sam laughed. "It was a spur of the moment thing."

"If dat's di story yuh telling …"

Sam bit her lip to prevent more laughter from escaping. She'd really annoyed her sister this time, so she tried soothing her. "Mish, trust me, if I had planned anything resembling a vacation, I would have called you. This happened suddenly."

"So yuh say," she grumbled. "So, where are you and Uncle Ted staying?"

Sam deliberately kept her answer vague and leaned her hip against the wooden railing. Kingston's corded muscles glistened in the early morning sunlight as he swam another lap. Watching him distracted Sam, who smiled in appreciation and waved when he flipped onto his back and floated with his legs spread apart and his hands folded behind his head.

He blew her a kiss and she had to focus her mind on the conversation. "Um, Ocho Rios."

"How long yuh goin' to be here?"

Pulling in a deep breath, Sam enjoyed one last eyeful of Kingston then walked inside the bedroom and sat cross-legged on the mattress. "A week or so."

"I miss yuh."

That was the last thing she expected Michele to say. "Awwww, sis. After all this time?"

"In case yuh forget, we haven't Facetimed in more dan two weeks."

"That's true. I'm sorry." That reminded Sam she also hadn't talked to Evita in a while. When they spoke again, Evita would joke that she was sending "divorce papers" to officially end their friendship. That's if she still thought of Sam as a friend.

"Riiight." Michele dragged the word out, then continued, "Yuh refused to answer my Facetime, but picked up di regular call."

"It's a long story," Sam offered, staring at the television screen.

"Try me," Michele said. "I'm listenin'."

Information was the highest currency in Sam's world. She didn't give it away unless forced to, and saying anything to Michele about Ted would be like telling a town crier. If the family found out about his situation via cable television, she'd answer then. For now, she'd keep her mouth shut. Ted's business wasn't hers to tell anyway.

"It's nothing you'd be interested in."

"Does it have to do wid Kingston?"

She pictured her sister's dark eyes narrowed with curiosity as she coiled slender fingers around her dark, curly hair that was a stark contrast to Sam's blonde tresses.

"Yes and no." She chuckled, then responded in the local lingo. "Mind yuh business."

"Since yuh not goin' to tell me nutten and because mi have a early meeting wid a client, dis is goodbye."

"Love you, sis."

"If yuh come back dis way, let's link up … even if it's not in dis house."

Michele's serious tone tugged at Sam's heartstrings and she sighed. "Sure. Tell Mom and Papa I love them."

She dropped the phone on the bed and headed for the shower, assessing the last forty-eight hours. If Ted wondered why she was avoiding him, he hadn't risked approaching her to ask. He'd been closeted in his study for most of each day, as far as she knew. In the evenings, she arrived at dinner just in time to be sure she didn't have to sit close to him. Her reaction might seem childish, but she needed distance to work through her emotions as she processed the data she'd discovered. She believed in forgiveness, but she wasn't handing it out before knowing Ted's position.

Only God knew where he stood in all the dishonest dealings conducted by MiVaxx. How could scientists, who were supposed to work for the betterment of mankind, produce harmful substances to do the opposite?

When your conscience is at odds with who God created you to be, these are the things that happen.

Kingston's words reverberated in her head and brought a wry smile to her lips. That man had so much wisdom. Her mind was unsettled after talking with Michele, but she wouldn't get stuck on family matters she didn't know how to resolve.

After slipping into jeans and a tee-shirt and putting her hair into a bun, she headed downstairs. In the kitchen, she greeted Miss Violet and stole a fried dumpling before heading out to the patio.

From the elevated deck, she watched first Hassan, then Ryan prowling along the perimeter of the property. To the casual observer, the two would appear to be out for an early-morning walk but she knew better. The sight of them brought back the reality she would rather have avoided.

When the housekeeper summoned her to the dining room, she met Kingston just outside the door. "Man, you're quick. Weren't you just in the pool?"

"Mmm-hmm, but this time I didn't have you to mess around with." The smirk left his lips as Kingston swept his thumb over her cheek and met her eyes. "How did you sleep?"

"Well enough," she lied, not wanting to start their interaction with tales of how her mind had wandered all night from one scenario to another involving her uncle. Or, the distrust around his takeover of her story. "I'm good."

"You don't look as if you rested enough."

"Trust me. I'm fine."

Kingston opened his mouth, but her uncle greeted them in the doorway. He sat at one end of the oval table and watched as Sam positioned herself on the other side of Kingston, away from him.

Today, Violet and her assistant had whipped up an American breakfast of eggs, bacon, sausages, toast, and waffles with pancake syrup. The delicious aroma of Blue Mountain coffee wafted from the percolator on the sideboard.

Hassan's appearance gave Sam an excuse to focus elsewhere as she asked how he liked the island so far.

"I love the little I've seen, but I look forward to catching a few sights while I'm here."

"We do have many interesting places for tourists to visit," Ted offered while sipping orange juice.

"Maybe when I visit again, I'll have the luxury of doing all the things tourists do. This time, it's about keeping you and your family safe."

When Sam's gaze met Ted's, she ignored the hurt in his eyes but couldn't help looking back at him when he said, "I was thinking we could go out later today. If I stay inside one more day, I'll go stir crazy."

"That might not be the wisest thing to do," Ryan warned on his way into the room. "Especially when you have enemies that aren't out in the open."

"I have some business in Trelawny." Ted shoved one hand through his thinning hair. "Nobody knows we're here. All of us can go. It would give us a break from being cooped up on the property."

When no one spoke, he continued, "We'd all be together, so the two of you would still be in proximity."

In the heavy silence, Ted added, "Trelawny is a safe place. And like I said, we'll all be together."

Sam exchanged a worried look with Kingston, who focused on Ted. "The only way I'll agree to this is if you get two additional security guards. It's unfair to these men to do what you're proposing without the added help."

Picking up his phone, her uncle said, "That won't be a problem."

Despite his assurance and chipper mood, the atmosphere in the room was thick with tension.

While Ted arranged added security based on Ryan's recommendation, Hassan and Ryan conversed in low tones.

Kingston, sensing her uneasiness, murmured words of comfort but Sam couldn't help speculating. What business did Ted have that was so important, when days ago he had no plans to be on the island?

Chapter 20

The John crows, or turkey buzzards, soaring overhead raised the hairs on the back of Kingston's neck. They only came around when dead meat was nearby, or when it was about to rain, but the sky was cloudless. According to his grandmother, when they settled on the roof of a house, someone who lived there would die. He pushed that thought away and threaded his fingers through Sam's soft hair.

Around them, the vegetation on both sides of the Martha Brae River reflected the signature green tinge of the water. Sam's gaze was fixed on the trees as the thirty-foot bamboo raft headed downstream. Their captain, Anthony, skillfully steered while telling them about the plant life and pointing out several varieties of birds, including woodpeckers that kept up a racket as they sailed by, barely creating ripples on the water. At the same time, he divided their attention by carving a small replica of a raft out of a gourd, all while talking.

Sam nuzzled his jaw, then whispered, "Are you feeling any better about this?"

Kingston flexed the muscles in his shoulders. "Not really. I think your uncle is reckless. Being stir crazy has made him lose perspective, not to mention a handle on reality."

She squeezed his thigh. "I kinda understand his position. It's hard staying locked up when you're home and want to be out and about."

"This is my home, too, but safety is common sense."

"The truth is, I was worried earlier until I realized he simply wanted to meet with the agent who oversees his properties on this side of the island. Stop worrying, we'll be fine. Ted and I are safe and we'll remain that way."

He didn't comment, but told himself that perhaps he was being apprehensive for no reason. Maybe that story being released was giving him the heebie-jeebies. Ted's blackmailers had failed to get the financial reward they wanted, so went ahead with blasting their information all over the news. What more would they do if they didn't get the money they'd been demanding?

"You know this is the parish where Usain Bolt was born?" Anthony asked.

Sam met Kingston's eyes and they burst into laughter.

"Yeah man," Sam answered, "we know dat."

Anthony blinked twice at her slip into Patios.

She hadn't spoken more than a few words, so Anthony didn't realize she was Jamaican. Kingston was aware that Sam took it in stride because she was used to being thought of as a foreigner because of her appearance. In a country where people of African descent made up more than seventy-six percent of the population, most gave her a second and third look when they heard her accent. Even now, Sam didn't like being singled out because of her olive skin.

When Kingston looked at her, he didn't see any of that, only the woman he loved. He used his forearm to turn Sam's head and grazed her lips with his. She was the center of his world in this moment.

Yet his mind traveled to the past without his permission. He'd had an easier time because of his darker skin and oriental features, but he'd also taken his fair share of ribbing in school. The insensitive jokes about eating dog meat had irked his soul, but he'd never shared his feelings with his mother, who would have been outraged. Jamaica might be a melting pot of races, but people did not observe political correctness. Nor did they care whether their words were hurtful to those who didn't share their similarities.

Every Chinese was Miss Chin, every Indian was described as a Coolie, and every man with dark skin was called "Blacks" or "Blacka". A woman with a light complexion was nicknamed "Browning." He'd been called Mr. Chin more than a few times. Because he understood the way of the people, by the time he reached adulthood, the misnomer didn't bother him. He couldn't do anything about his racial makeup. Kingston was simply the result of his parents' genetic codes and proud to be their son.

His parents went to separate Catholic high schools and met on a Ministry program during a visit to a golden age home, where they cared for the residents. Their relationship developed as they walked home after school each afternoon, then blossomed when their educational path took them to teachers' colleges. Years later, armed with their teaching degrees, they went to work overseas. When they returned home, they settled in Montego Bay to raise their son. As time passed, familial opposition helped them decide to migrate to the United States.

"How long did they say the ride would last?" Sam asked, trailing her fingers through the water.

"Just over an hour," Kingston said as his mind returned to the present, "and we're past that now."

Sam pointed to the raft ahead of them where Ted sat with Ryan, who continued to scan both banks of the river. "He doesn't look as if he's enjoying this either."

With a wry grin, Kingston said, "The man's job is security and we've made his assignment twice as hard with this trip Ted just *had* to take."

"You have to admit it's more fun than going straight back to the villa."

"True, but I'll be more at ease when I know we're within the confines of four walls, with technology to assist if I need it."

"You are such a kill-joy."

"Nah, just super cautious." He touched his lips to Sam's forehead. "Especially when it concerns my woman."

"Awww, that's so sweet." Sam closed her eyes and turned her face up to the sun. She looked like a child without a care in the world and he'd do all he could to keep things that way.

"You could make it sweeter by not going on that China trip," she said after a moment.

Her words jolted him, and he sighed. "If you slowed down sometimes, you'd find the answers you're seeking, but—"

"What are you talking about?"

Kingston caressed her shoulder as he grinned. "For days, I've been trying to tell you that I've reconsidered the timing, and maybe—"

Her knees bumped his. "So, you're not going?"

"Let's finish this discussion later." He tipped his chin toward Anthony. "Our captain wants to say something."

"Do you know how the river got its name?" Anthony asked, glancing over his shoulder.

"No, please tell us," Sam answered.

In her ear, Kingston whispered, "The name Martha Brae is a corruption of the name the Spanish gave the river, Rio Mateberion. I found that out from the internet."

"Shush, I prefer the romanticized version."

Anthony lifted his voice and began his tale. "Legend says Martha was a Taino Indian and a witch. De Spanish people who settled here tortured her to reveal to dem where she hid a chest full of gold along the river. After telling dem, she used magic to change the river course, so dey couldn't find di gold. After dat, she sealed di cave entrance where she hid di gold." Antonio enjoyed a belly laugh. "Up to today nobody find dat gold yet."

Sam chuckled with him, but Kingston was still uneasy without knowing why. Behind them, Hassan and the security guard seemed uncomfortable. Both men scoured the landscape with their eyes, and Kingston could well understand why.

As they approached their destination, he should have felt relieved but was more on edge. His instincts had kept him safe in more dangerous parts of the world, and he had no reason to doubt himself now. He tightened his arm around Sam, wanting nothing more than to exit the raft, which left them wide open to attack.

Ahead of them, Ryan swept a hand across Ted's chest and shouted, "Get down!"

Kingston's gaze zeroed in on the bank and he rose in a half-crouch. The moment he heard the first blast, he spun Sam to his other side, which launched them into the water. Seconds after another report and a flash from the berth, Ted yelled as Ryan grabbed him and dove into the river.

Screams echoed among those standing on the berth and people ran in every direction.

With Sam shielded behind him and one arm around his neck, Kingston watched the gunman casually walk toward the front of the property amidst the chaos.

Anthony, who surfaced beside them, asked, "Di two o' yuh all right?"

"I'm good," Kingston said, while Ryan pulled Ted from the water.

Hassan and the security guard with him moved through the crowd toward the exit.

When Kingston asked what was going on, Ryan said, "Our second man is nowhere in sight. I believe he took off after the shooter. The arrangement was for him to meet us, here at the dock."

After smoothing the soaked hair away from Sam's face, Kingston cupped her cheeks. "Are you okay, babe?"

"Yes, I am." Sam looked down and her face went ashen as she gasped. "Kingston, you've been shot."

Chapter 21

No matter how hard she fought, Sam's thoughts overrode her will. Her mind kept replaying the moment when Kingston had snatched her and plunged them into the water. Something about the attack on the group teased the edges of her consciousness. The series of events didn't add up, but she was stymied.

Thank God Kingston is still alive.

They had just made the two-hour trip from Montego Bay and were back inside the villa with Ryan and one other security guard. Despite Ryan's reassurance that the two new additions were not under suspicion, Sam was leery and asked that the stranger be stationed outside the villa.

Ryan, bless his heart, switched things up and allowed her to have her way. "We'll do as you ask," he'd said.

Until she understood what was at work, anyone new to the picture was suspect. She trusted Ryan and Hassan only because they'd been assigned to them by the Kings of the Castle and she'd done background research on them and found out they were all upstanding men who gave back to their communities through their action and affluence.

From the bed, where she was propped against the bedhead, she gazed through the plate glass at the sky's red and orange hues. Next to her, Kingston frowned at his computer screen. The bandaid sleeve over his wound reminded her that his injury could have been much worse. She couldn't see what he was working on without craning her neck, and to her surprise, resentment crept back to bother her.

"I can feel you staring at me," Kingston said as his mouth curved into that half smile she adored.

"I'm just grateful you weren't killed because of me or my family. I can't help it."

He winced, then positioned himself so he could stroke her cheek with his thumb. "Feed your mind with good thoughts, Sam. Both of us could have been shot, but we're okay. Give thanks."

"Trust me, I am, but—" Her gaze slid toward the laptop screen, but she forced herself to meet his gaze.

"Shhh." He sealed her lips with one finger, then touched her damp hair. "I'm all right. Your uncle will be right as rain in a few days. And you're just a teeny-bit waterlogged."

They both chuckled over his comment, then she kissed his palm. "Yes, God has been good to us."

The gunshot had gone straight through Kingston's outer arm and the doctor had closed the wound with stitches and applied bandages. Try as she might, Sam couldn't avoid thinking that the bullet was meant for her. If Kingston hadn't moved into the line of fire, only God knew if she would have survived being hit.

Ted hadn't been as fortunate as Kingston. Despite Ryan's efforts, Ted took a bullet to the shoulder. Although he insisted he didn't want to stay in the private hospital overnight, the doctor gave him no choice. After giving a statement to the police, Ted, Kingston, and Ryan agreed that Hassan and the other guard would remain at the hospital and travel to Ocho Rios with Ted the following morning. She prayed nothing else would happen by the time he left Montego Bay.

"D'you think my uncle knows more than he's admitting?" she asked.

"Hard to say." Kingston stroked his jaw, which now had a sexy growth of stubble. "He looked shaken, which is a pretty good indication that everything took him by surprise."

Sam pulled her knees up and wrapped her arms around them. "I hope the Kings get to the bottom of the business with Hardy. With friends like that, Ted doesn't need any enemies."

"For real." Kingston shook his head, "But like my grandmother used to say, if you lay with dogs, you rise with fleas."

Sam's phone rang and she picked it up off the bedside table. "Hey, Michele, what's up?"

"Yuh know you're something else?" her sisters said in a querulous tone.

"A greeting would be in order since we haven't spoken for a few days, but why d'you say that?" Sam plumped the pillow behind her and leaned back.

"I have to hear on di news dat you almost got killed?"

"What?" Sam squeaked and sat up.

"Yes, someone captured di shooting dat took place dis afternoon at Martha's Rest. I saw you and Caramel King on de video loop."

Glancing at Kingston, she snapped, "Stop calling him that."

"Right now, dat's neither here nor dere. And by di way, where di heck are you?"

Cautiously, Sam replied, "In Ochi."

"The news report said people got shot." Michele's voice climbed by several decibels, which earned Sam a concerned glance from Kingston. "Who did?"

Sam settled on the pillows with a sigh, knowing Michele would keep asking questions until she was satisfied. "Ted and Kingston."

"How is Uncle Ted?" Michele squawked. "Is he all right?"

"Still at a private facility."

"When dey plan to release him, and is he wounded bad?"

"What are you, a consulting physician?" Sam asked, then patted Kingston's leg when he raised both brows.

"Don't be feisty. You're not his only niece. I'm concerned about my uncle."

"I'm sorry. I forgot you don't have these details." Sam wiggled to make herself comfortable, then continued, "The gunshot went through his shoulder, above his collar bone. Based on the angle of entry they had to find and remove bits of bone. Plus his blood pressure was elevated. He was subdued when we left but other than that, he should be fine."

"Sounds like Ted and Kingston got off easy."

Shaking her head, Sam quipped, "Well, if you can call having your collar bone nearly shattered getting off easy …"

"Yuh know what I mean. T'ank God nutten more serious happened."

Frowning, Sam asked, "How is Papa recuperating?"

"You want de truth or de fairy-tale edition?"

Sam got off the bed to walk around the room. "He's acting like he's lost his mind, isn't he?"

"If he was affecting only himself dat would be one thing, but he's driving Mom to her limit. You know she has no control over him."

"And what are you doing to help?" Sam asked, perching on a stool next to the vanity. In the mirror, her eyes reflected annoyance.

"Staying out of di way. You know my policy. I keep a low profile around here."

"Michele, if you're in the house and he's being difficult don't you think it would make things easier for her if—"

"Don' preach to me," she yelled. "You know our father. Only God can intervene when him start actin' like di devil."

Her gaze met Kingston's, but the crease to his brow told Sam he was far away. She wrapped up the call, promising to ring Michele tomorrow with an update. When she rose, Kingston spoke.

"Where did you say Evita was stationed this time around?"

"Liberia, why?"

"That's the place some of the MiVaxx investors have in common." When she tipped her head sideways, he said, "A few of them anyway."

"Actually, I've been thinking about contacting her, despite what I said before." She climbed back into the bed to sit cross-legged in front of him. "Why does it sound as if you know more than you've told me?"

"Not really. I'm just saying it might be useful to talk to her. This vaccine we've been looking at has been sold to that country and remember they've had several outbreaks of Ebola."

"And if we have someone on the ground there, then ..." She waved one hand, encouraging Kingston to complete her sentence.

"We may be able to access first-hand information about the side-effects."

"The only hitch we have is that Liberia is five hours ahead of Jamaica." She bit one corner of her lip. "But technology knows no borders, so I'll send her a message to say we need to speak with her face to face on whatever platform is convenient."

"In the meantime, let me get hold of Trey-Jon. Something just occurred to me."

Sam closed the cover of the laptop, moved it to the other side of the bed, and kneeled in front of Kingston. "I know you're in investigative mode, but after today's excitement, I need you to hold me."

As their breath mingled, Kingston whispered, "Are you sure that's all you're after?"

She couldn't help the wicked smile that came to her lips. "If not, I'm sure you're ready to supply all my needs."

Kingston dropped soft kisses along the side of her neck as he whispered, "Just say the word, Samantha. You know I aim to please."

Chapter 22

"He planned his own kidnapping?" Kingston's eyebrows rose, then settled when he glanced at Sam. Her stormy eyes conveyed not only anger, but disbelief.

"I'm sorry, but I have to ask," Kingston leaned closer to the screen. "How do we know these demands on Ted DaCosta are legit?"

Trey-Jon twirled a pen between two fingers and smiled broadly before he said, "Remember I was telling you about the company Hardy keeps? Well, he's been in conversation with certain persons that DaCosta isn't privy to and doesn't know."

"And the subject of these conversations?"

"This is the part where I tell you that you're asking too many questions." Trey-Jon's lopsided grin took the sting out of his words. "These older guys may be slick but they don't understand that technology has a way of giving up their secrets."

Kingston didn't press him because aside from never revealing exactly how he got information, they couldn't speak as freely as they normally did with Sam present. He had a feeling Trey-Jon was holding something back, but he'd wait until they could have a private conversation to find out what else he knew. At that time, Kingston would sift through whatever information he received before sharing it with Sam, especially if Ted was in trouble they didn't yet know about.

Glancing between them, Sam puckered her mouth. "Trey-Jon, there's something you're not saying. Just know I'm on to you two."

He held up both hands. "You know how it is."

"Yes. I'm in the loop on a need-to-know basis. Anyway, I may not want to be privy to whatever it is you're holding back." Leaning closer, Sam focused closely on the screen. "I'm not sure if you're still in touch with Evita, but we wanted to talk with her. Since that conversation is pertinent to this one, do you mind if we add her? Or would you prefer if—"

"No, it's fine."

Trey-Jon dragged a hand across his face, which told Kingston he was uncomfortable, so he said, "We can do this after—"

"No, man, I said it was fine." Trey-Jon softened his voice and raised one hand. "It's okay. Really."

Evita and Trey-Jon had been close while they were at the university, but had abruptly ended their relationship. Kingston had suspected, but never confirmed the reason for the split. If they hadn't been in touch over the years, meeting like this would be a shock for both of them.

Kingston glanced at Sam, whose smile was reassuring. "Let me add her to this call."

They exchanged banter about Kingston getting back stateside in one piece until Evita appeared onscreen. She was a beautiful woman, who wore her hair in cornrows that ended in a large afro at the back. Evita hadn't changed much since they had been in school, and wore the same brilliant smile. "Hello, everyone. Long time no see."

Aside from a greeting and saying he now worked in technology, Trey-Jon was unnaturally quiet. His gaze kept shifting to and from the screen, as though the sight of Evita was painful.

"So, Evita, as Sam told you, we wanted to find out about the Ebzirton vaccine." Kingston cleared his throat. "We know it has a high efficacy rate, but also want to find out what you saw on the job."

"The first thing is that the doctors I've been working with refused to use it once they realized it had harmful effects." She grimaced, then continued, "The government health minister that touted Ebzirton was eventually disgraced and forced to resign. Apparently, he got some kickback from allowing the drug to be used here."

"Did he go to prison?" Trey-Jon asked, frowning.

With a faint smile, Evita shook her head. "In third world countries, things don't always work the same way as in our society. Give it a few years and people forget. He'll probably be back seeking re-election in another year or so."

"So, about those side-effects," Sam prompted while propping her cheek on one hand.

"Where do I start?" Evita asked, staring at the bottom of the screen. "Anxiety, depression, organ failure, sterility, death. And those are the ones that come to mind right away. And by the way, the last three I mentioned are not on the package inserts as known risks."

Kingston scribbled on a pad, then tipped his head toward the screen. "So, wouldn't the health ministry have reported these side effects to the lab once the doctors there recognized the dangers?"

Evita glanced to her right before she said, "When you have crooked people in authority, it takes a while before they listen to any outcry from health workers who realize the drug isn't working the way it should."

"Do you know if any compensation has been paid to the government by the manufacturer?" Trey-Jon asked.

Evita shook her head. "That's hard to say. The whole thing has been hush-hush. I only know all this because I was part of the team that has been on the ground the longest."

Glancing at Sam, who frowned as he took notes, Kingston said, "That's part of the problem. They do their dirt, keep everything on the QT, then peddle their poison elsewhere."

"That's right." Trey-Jon nodded. "From what I found, they've sold that same poison to other African countries."

After Sam's gaze strayed to the guard downstairs, she released a tiny sigh. "Evita, thanks so much. Let's talk again without the men, okay?"

Her friend smiled, then agreed, "Let's do that."

Evita's gaze shifted. "It's been good seeing you again, Trey-Jon."

"Good talking to you, too." For a couple of seconds, he said nothing, then mumbled, "Let's talk again, okay?"

She nodded. "I'd like that. 'Bye."

Once the call ended, Sam cupped one hand under her jaw. "This story is all kinds of complicated. It means more research, plus I'll have to ask Evita for permission to use what she told me."

"Agreed. I'm going to share what I know with the Kings and see how best we can end this situation with your uncle and whoever is behind the blackmail and attack."

"This is such a tangled mess." Sam got to her feet and returned to Kingston's bedroom.

He followed her inside and pulled her into a hug. "How about we get something to eat then tackle what we have to do?"

Slipping both hands around his waist, Sam laid her head against his chest. "Sounds like a good plan to me."

A second later, Sam met his gaze. "By the way, that's the first time I can ever recall Trey-Jon being tongue-tied. Like he didn't know what to say."

"Mmmm. He really liked her, but I totally understand him not wanting to be pushy."

Wriggling her eyebrows, Sam asked, "D'you think they'll get it together and have that conversation?"

Kingston kissed her forehead, then murmured, "They're older and wiser, so I believe so."

The ringing of her phone was loud in the quiet room. Sam groaned, then asked, "Who could be calling this early?"

While she went back to the balcony, Kingston picked up the remote and switched on the television. Sam's sharp tone demanded his attention.

"Where did you hear that?" She stepped inside and held on to the doorframe. "What newsflash?"

She threw a panicked look at Kingston, then said, "I have to make a call. Talk later."

Kingston met Sam halfway and gripped her arms. "What happened?"

"There was a shoot-out at the hospital. Michele said there was a news clip on the radio." She closed her eyes, then added, "Someone was killed but they haven't released the person's identity."

Chapter 23

"Think about this." Sam paced the living room and stopped in front of the seat Ted occupied. "While you're keeping secrets, people are being killed."

He raised one arm, then winced and rubbed his forehead with his other hand. "I don't know why anyone would want me dead."

"Have those men contacted you again about paying them?" she snapped.

He shrugged and contorted his face. "It wouldn't make sense since they already went through with their threats. Besides, my phone hasn't stopped ringing since the story broke, so I had to turn it off."

"Let me ask you this." Kingston had leaned against the wall near the entrance, listening to the conversation. "Who did you tell that we were coming to Jamaica? Sam told me it was on the news that you were headed to the Caribbean, but the announcer didn't say where."

"That's an excellent question." Ryan nodded from the large sofa while Hassan studied each of their faces, as if hunting for clues.

Hands to her hips, Sam stopped adjacent to Ted. "You may as well tell us because none of this is going away."

When he stayed silent, she glared at him. "Obviously, you don't give a damn about anyone else, but don't you care that people are getting hurt around you? Kingston could have been killed because of whatever stupid game you're playing. Hassan and the other security guard were almost casualties. For heaven's sake, spare a thought for someone other than yourself."

"I honestly don't know what this is about." He stared across the room, then added, "The only person I told was Hardy."

"Now I know for sure you have a death wish." Sam's gaze shot to Kingston, who walked farther into the room to sit on the adjacent sofa.

Kingston rubbed his jaw and narrowed his eyes. "Are you for real? Why are you still in contact with him?"

"We've been friends for a long time." Ted's tone was defensive, even as Kingston shook his head.

"The truth is that your friend arranged his own kidnapping."

Ted gasped and his skin blanched. "That can't be true."

"Take my word for it," Kingston said. "My source is reliable."

"B-but he didn't know about me being in the hospital. He couldn't have." A tense silence hung in the cool, elegant space before Ted choked out his next words. "I didn't tell him that."

"Well, someone's definitely behind this. Who could it be?" Ryan stood and walked to the far window, dialing a number on his cell phone. "The other man we caught wouldn't say a word about who sent him. The police might have loosened his lips by now. I also know Dro and Daron will be working on Hardy at their end."

A glance at Ted made Sam take a second look. Now, he was gray around the lips at the mention of The Fixer and the Tech Guru from The Castle. The anxiety and confusion in his eyes were obvious.

"You need to lie down." She peered at him, wishing she knew how to unravel the mess he'd created. "Have you eaten?"

"Yes, just before we drove here."

"Let's get you to your bedroom. Are you strong enough to go upstairs, or should I get Violet to help me?"

"The gunshot didn't turn me into a vegetable. I'll be fine." He stood, then said in a gentle tone, "I'm sorry. I know you're only trying to help."

She nodded but didn't speak as she walked by his side and escorted him upstairs. At the door to his bedroom, she touched his arm. "Please, if there's anything you haven't told us, now is a great time since we're all stumbling around in the darkness."

With a hand to her cheek, he said, "I'm sorry about all of this. If I remember anything, you and Kingston will be the first to know."

His haggard face roused her affection and sympathy. Gently, she hugged him avoiding the bandage on his shoulder. In his ear, she whispered, "I love you, you old troublemaker."

He patted her back. "I love you, too, Sunshine."

Sam's eyes watered because he hadn't called her that in years. He might be driving her mad right now, but she loved Ted as if he were her father. She often wished he were, but would never admit it to anyone, especially her parents.

When the door closed between them, she waited a moment before pulling back her shoulder and returning downstairs. The thought of losing him or Kingston didn't bear thinking about. He had all but confirmed he wasn't taking that China trip now, but it still beat against the edges of her consciousness. She prayed good sense would keep him from flying across the world when they had only just moved past a pandemic that still threatened the world.

The men had disappeared from the living area, but she tracked their voices to the dining room, where they had set up several laptops. An unidentified device rested on the table between Hassan and Ryan. Without asking, she knew it was a communication tool. If her instinct was right, it was a secure internet connection that would keep their discussion private.

She slid into the seat next to Kingston and glanced at his laptop. The men she'd met from The Castle were onscreen—Daron, Dro, Jai, Shaz, Vikkas, plus the security experts, Nicco and Angela.

"Could it be that there may be a tracking device on Ted, his vehicle, or his personal possessions that is allowing these people to pinpoint his location wherever he goes?" Jai asked.

"The easiest way to do that would be with a cell phone," Daron said. "But if there is another kind of tracker, it would have to be specifically geared toward international use."

"And it would mean the person had advance knowledge that Ted was leaving the country," Nicco added.

"Ted did say he told Hardy," Kingston chipped in.

Sam touched his arm, to get his attention. "But they didn't have time for person-to-person contact for him to put any kind of tracker in place."

"There is that, not that he couldn't get someone else to do it for him."

After staring at the painting on the opposite wall of a river overflowing its banks, Ryan looked at Hassan, then at Sam. "We'll have to check your uncle's room and possessions to eliminate the possibility that there's a tracking device somewhere in this house."

"As well as the cars," Hassan added.

"Good catch," Ryan said, tipping his head toward him.

"What about the two security guards?" Sam asked. "They're new on the scene, so …"

"I wouldn't bet my life on it, but I don't think they have anything to do with this. We're more than thorough in vetting the security personnel we use, no matter the country we're in. It's Castle protocol. Besides, I was in the Bahamas when Shaz asked me to fly over, so they were my first choice. I know the company and their operating standards. We've done business before."

Sam didn't like the direction in which her thoughts were trending. Each likely possibility was being shredded as incredible, which left one scenario. She wanted to speak to Kingston alone in the worst way, but didn't want to disrupt the meeting. What she needed to convey couldn't be shared with the men in the room and onscreen. Her thoughts were almost sacrilegious, but something in her gut said she shouldn't ignore her instincts. They had never steered her in the wrong direction.

Sharing her suspicions with Kingston would be painful, but she trusted him more than anyone else in this matter, even her sister at this point. She willed herself to sit still until the meeting ended.

Ryan's voice jolted Sam from her thoughts when he said, "That's good news."

"What happened?" she whispered in Kingston's ear.

"Hardy's been picked up by the Chicago police for questioning."

"Is that coming off the article in the paper?" Kingston asked.

"Not at this time," Vikkas replied, "but we believe that's coming down the pipeline. This time, it's on a charge of public mischief for his kidnapping stunt."

Grinning, Ryan said, "We have Kingston and his friend to thank for that bit of intel."

While the men organized themselves to do a complete sweep of the house for any tracking devices, including the bedrooms, Sam rehearsed the main item on her agenda. She had to convince Kingston to make the trip into the capital city with her tomorrow.

Chapter 24

The three-story house where Sam grew up was imposing. In daylight, the burnt-orange façade, decorative stonework, and terracotta roof tiles combined for a tasteful Spanish-style ambience.

In the backseat of the SUV, Kingston prepared himself for what he was sure would be high drama. Sam slipped her fingers between his and held on tight. He gave her a reassuring smile. "Everything will be fine. I know you can handle yourself."

"If you say so." Sam scanned the well-maintained garden, which was colorful and picturesque. The hybrid roses in pink, yellow, and white were eye-catching, but Sam looked at them as though their beauty hid some kind of rot that was invisible to the eye.

Ryan, and the security guard they now identified as Graham, stepped onto the driveway tiles and scanned their surroundings while they waited for the Mitsubishi Outlander carrying Ted, Hassan, and the other guard, Graves, to pull into the property. When the automatic gates swung shut behind the second vehicle, Kingston tipped Sam's chin toward him to look into her eyes. "You haven't told any of us why this trip was necessary, but we'll know in a few minutes, right?"

She freed her chin and nodded. "Thank you for trusting me and convincing the team to do this because I asked."

"After all that's happened …"

"You'll see it was necessary." Sam sighed and tapped the middle of her torso. "When your gut tells you something, you follow it. We both know all about that."

This time he dipped his head, his attention drawn to the open front door and Michele, who walked into the sunlight clad in jeans and a tee-shirt. Sam's smile at the sight of her sister was joyous, yet it carried a hint of sadness.

Graham held the door open, and she stepped out and ran across the tiles to hug Michele, who waved at Kingston over Sam's shoulder. When they stepped apart, he extended his hand, but Michele pulled him into a loose hug. "It's good to see yuh again. I doubt this visit will be any better than di last one, but I'm begging yuh to be patient wid Papa."

If he hadn't learned from last time, Michele's warm presence and her "local" sound pegged her as someone who was not impressed by her family or the position they held in society. She sounded like an ordinary Jamaican, who could go seamlessly from English to Patois, depending on the company she was with.

"We'll see how that goes," Kingston said. "I draw the line at him mistreating Sam."

Sam faced the house when her mother stepped onto the veranda.

Mrs. DaCosta's smile faded when she noticed him, but her reaction to Ted spiked Kingston's curiosity. Her color deepened before it seeped out of her face. She embraced Sam, then took several steps to Ted, who sandwiched her hands between his. The look they exchanged was hard to decipher but Kingston's sense of curiosity was heightened in more than one way.

Yesterday evening, after the online conference with the Kings, Sam had grown pensive. For a while, she watched him work in silence. Then she paced the living room and went for a walk in the yard. On returning, she said, "I have to go home in the morning."

When he raised both brows, she continued. "We *must* go into Kingston."

Technically, Sam's family lived in St. Andrew, but the two areas were combined as one parish—Kingston & St. Andrew—for municipal purposes.

She would not explain why the trip was urgent, which frustrated Kingston. While Ryan and Hassan swept the rest of the house for tracking devices, Sam kept the staff occupied in the kitchen chatting, and Kingston kept watch in the living room. While there, he'd been distracted by information Trey-Jon had sent through. What he'd failed to say in their online conference was that Hardy had more evil intentions for Ted, who was supposedly his friend.

At dinner time, when Ted appeared, Ryan had quietly excused himself to search for any tracking or listening device among Ted's personal possessions. The bug Daron had installed in his phone remained in place. Kingston doubted Ted remembered its existence after all the upheaval. Other than that, they found nothing. During the online meeting, the Kings confirmed that Ted had had no further contact with Hardy.

After Sam's stubborn non-disclosure of her reasons for seeing her family, Kingston had the task of convincing Ryan and Hassan to drive fifty miles to the DaCosta home. Eventually, the two men agreed, but Ryan warned, "This goes against everything I stand for as a security expert. My instincts and training tell me that we could be walking into another trap."

Hassan had smiled in a rueful way, then said, "I can't say I don't understand and identify with what Kingston is trying to achieve. Love will make you bend over backward to accommodate the woman of your heart."

"Not to mention go a million miles out of your way to keep her happy," Ryan added.

Chuckling, Kingston asked, "Isn't that saying the same thing in different words?"

"Being accommodating and keeping her happy aren't necessarily the same thing," Ryan answered, "But you'll learn that eventually, youngun' and I'm speaking as a man who's been married for several years."

"All of two." Hassan's tone was dry. "But love is love, be it ten years or just a couple years of bliss."

"And just how long have you been married to Blair?" Ryan asked, glancing at him.

With a grin, Hassan quipped, "Would you look at the time."

When Kingston laughed, Hassan went on to explain how he and Ryan had met while trying to locate his girlfriend, who'd been kidnapped in the Middle East.

Their exchange had amused Kingston, but he knew exactly what they meant. No other woman could have convinced him to stand by her side, knowing how her family felt about him. Today wouldn't be any different from the last time he was here. His gut told him so.

He followed the three women into the cool house. At the entrance to the living room, Sharon DaCosta ushered them to what she called the parlor.

Sam grimaced, and Kingston knew she was embarrassed. He could almost hear her thinking that her mother was pretentious. She'd told him that a time or two, among other things.

The rust-colored sofas and drapery in shades of orange complemented the pale tangerine walls. Such warm hues should have made the house welcoming, but the air-conditioning and Mrs. DaCosta's cool demeanor put Kingston on edge.

Their unexpected arrival had to be a surprise, but she acted unbothered. Only her shifting eyes gave away her discomfort. "Please make yourselves comfortable while I ask Elias to come downstairs."

Hassan, Ryan, Graham, and Graves engaged in a quick conversation, then the two guards returned to the front of the house. Dressed as they were in long-sleeved shirts with the cuffs rolled back and dark glasses, they appeared to have just left a meeting and had discarded their jackets. Kingston's lips quirked at the thought of the nineties sci-fi movie *Men in Black*, except this was no high-level comedy.

Lives were at stake and Kingston believed more was at work than they were seeing. With Hardy in custody and under investigation, he should have felt more relieved but something else was happening that he couldn't pinpoint. Why would local thugs be brought into the picture to harm Ted and Sam simply to collect money on a shakedown that hadn't paid off?

He sensed that whatever was driving Sam tied into this situation, but she wasn't ready to divulge anything. Her jaw was set, her hands clasped, and heat filled her gaze. Unlike other times, she did not seem to need the reassurance of their connection. Or maybe, she didn't want him touching her in her parents' presence. He pushed that sour thought away. Now wasn't the time to speculate on what didn't matter at this moment. Something deeper under the surface was at work in Sam's mind.

Michele returned to the room with Rose, the woman who had served them at dinner on his first visit. Both carried tumblers with what looked like fruit punch. They quickly laid out the coasters and glasses, then left the room. On her way back in, Michele entered at the same time as her father and mother, who appeared from the opposite direction. The two Shih Tzu accompanied them.

At first sight of Sam, Elias DaCosta allowed a tight smile to escape from him, then his attention moved to Ted and Kingston. He scowled, then studied Hassan and Ryan before a frown descended. His thick brows pulled toward each other and his gaze shot to Sam. "What's the meaning of this? You couldn't get away from the hospital fast enough. Then we don't hear from you for days, and now you're back."

He positioned himself on the seat as if he were a king receiving his subjects, and laid pudgy hands on the padded chair arms, without acknowledging anyone else in the room. "To what do we owe the pleasure of this visit?" Elias' snarky tone could not be mistaken for anything other than what it was—an insult.

Cool in a white, halter-top blouse and a gold skirt that covered her ankles, Sam uncrossed her legs. She sat so that her red-painted toes peeked out from under the soft material. "This visit is anything but a pleasure ... Father."

Mr. DaCosta's skin flushed. "So, we're back to that."

Sam hiked one shoulder. "If you insist on treating me the way you do ..."

Scowling harder, he ground out through his teeth, "What do you want?"

"Facts." Samantha said, with no inflection to her words. "It's the currency I deal in. Cold. Hard. Facts."

Opening his arms wide, Elias said, "How can I help you?" as if speaking to a stranger.

Sam's gaze slid to her sister, who watched from an adjacent seat. Meanwhile, Sharon petted one of the dogs that climbed onto the sofa.

"I find it curious that Ted and I arrived here and everything was fine until *you*."

He sputtered. "Wh-What are you trying to say?"

"Only *thi*s family knew we were on the island." Sam looked at Kingston as if to say her mention of the media knowing they were in the area didn't matter. "As soon as we were out and about, the attacks started."

"So what does that have to do with me?" Elias asked with his eyebrows almost touching his sparse hair.

Sam walked around the room, then looked at Ted, who sat forward with his hands locked together. "Who else would know that Ted only owns two properties in Ocho Rios?"

She allowed the silence to stretch before she continued, "If we were not staying at one, we had to be at the other."

Kingston, Hassan, and Ryan exchanged glances then focused on Sam, who stopped behind her sister's seat. He now understood where this trip was headed.

"I told Michele we were staying in Ochi."

Her sister gasped and turned in the seat. "What yuh really saying? Yuh crazy if yuh t'ink I would do anyt'ing to hurt yuh."

"I'm not accusing you of anything." Her fiery eyes settled on Elias. "Once, I could overlook, but when Michele and I spoke again, I told her Ted was staying at a private hospital. Since there are very few of them in MoBay, it would have been easy for a resourceful person, such as yourself, to pin down his location."

The two DaCosta men stared at each other. Their skin was pasty, and the resemblance between them startling.

Sharon put a trembling hand to her throat, while Michele's lips were parted and her pupils dilated.

When Sam spoke again, her voice was so low everyone in the room strained to hear her words. "I racked my brain over everything that happened in the last three to four days. And you know what I think?"

While she examined each face, a tide of color crept up her neck to flush her cheeks. She inhaled deeply, then released her breath. "Father, *you* sent those men to kill your brother."

Chapter 25

Sam's anger spilled over and she yelled, "Why would you do something so wicked to your own flesh and blood?"

Elias gripped the end of the chair arms and narrowed his eyes. "Are you asking me, or are you telling me I've done this?"

"I'm not asking you anything. Just informing you of what I see in front of me." She smoothed her hair with one hand and laid the other on the glass shelving with a display of family portraits. "I've been studying this from all angles and cannot fathom why you would hire someone to kill not only your brother, but your child."

With everyone's attention on the two of them, Elias ground his teeth as his skin reddened to the pale crimson shade of an unripe otaheite apple. She hadn't eaten one of the sweet, home-grown fruit in years, and her father's deepening color—which reminded her of it—was alarming.

Sam feared he would have another heart attack, but that might be best for all of them. She sank onto the seat next to Kingston, but didn't look away from her father. "Well, aren't you going to say anything? You at least owe it to me to explain why."

"I don't know how you can accuse your father of such a terrible act." Sharon's voice was strangled, but Sam was past mollycoddling any of her parents.

"I've just added the clues together and—"

"Came up with an outrageous number," Elias blustered and glared at Sharon, as if she should have better control of her daughter. "The nerve."

"I dare to have a lot of nerve because I know I'm on to something." She stared at Elias, ignoring the steel in his eyes. "Tell me Michele didn't share that information with you. After that, I'll rest my case and apologize. If you want."

"It will take more than an apology for you to repair the damage you've done." Elias stood and pointed at Sam. "You've gone too far this time, don't you ever—"

"For heaven's sake, Elias," Sharon snapped. "Sit down and shut up."

Sam and Michele exchanged an incredulous look while their father continued posturing.

Eyes closed, Sharon put a hand to her forehead. "Elias, please stop," she said in a calmer tone. "You're only making yourself look like an idiot, plus giving me a headache."

"What are you talking about, woman?" He shook as he sat, ruffling his hair with clumsy fingers. "All of you have lost your minds and *you* have forgotten your place."

"It's over, Elias. There's no need to—"

Elias snarled, leaning toward Sharon. "You don't get to tell me what to say, or do, or how to act, you hear me?"

"You're not the boss of this body, Elias DaCosta," Sharon spat, rearing forward so far that the dog scrabbled off her lap to join the one on the floor. "I do have a mind of my own."

Again, Sam looked at Michele, who frowned at their parents. "Could someone explain to me what just happened? I'm as confused as a fart in a wicker chair dat can't find its way out."

Hassan and Ryan tried to hold back their smiles while Kingston's lips twitched, but his amusement faded when Elias pointed at Ted, then Sharon. "Ask the two of them. Maybe they can tell you."

Elias sank in the seat behind him, massaging his chest. The action was as false as a promise made in a state of desperation.

Neither Ted nor Sharon looked up or attempted to answer Michele's question.

"Here we go again," Michele muttered, then sat up like a jack-in-the-box. "For di love of all dat is holy, can someone enlighten my darkness?"

When no one spoke, Elias squared his shoulders. He waggled a finger between Michele and himself. "Apparently, you and I are the only jokers in this card pack."

"What?" Wrinkling her nose, Michele tipped her head sideways. "Yuh not helping mi to understand what's at play here, Papa."

He sat up and draped both arms over the sides of the chair. "Since I came home from hospital, I've been putting things in order. A heart attack makes you think about your mortality."

The soft droning of the air-conditioner was the only disturbance to the silence that blanketed the room.

"So," Elias continued, "I was going through some documents. Birth papers. Vaccination records. Things like that."

Michele propped her chin on her knuckles, watching her father's every movement.

"When I looked at Sam's history, I noticed her blood type. Now, I wasn't the most brilliant boy in school but in my mind, some things are impossible. So, Type O blood, plus another Type O donor will produce a child that is also Type O. I did an internet search to be sure I was right. Turned out I was."

Swallowing hard, Sam gripped Kingston's hand, which he turned over to join with hers. Before, she had been secure in the knowledge that her father was a snake. Now, he was showing his fangs and was poised to strike. The queasiness in her stomach said the result would be bad.

Elias glowered at their linked hands as if offended, but Sam didn't care and held on tighter.

Throwing a glare at Sharon, Elias continued his story. "Somehow, though, my wife and I managed to produce a miracle, because my older daughter does *not* have my blood type."

To soothe the tremor in Sam's arm, Kingston stroked her skin. She didn't acknowledge his gesture, she was too focused on what her father was about to share.

Pointing to Hassan and Ryan, Kingston said, "Perhaps we should leave the family alone while you talk about these things."

"Oh no, Kingdom, Kingston, or whatever your name is." Elias' eyes sparkled with spite. "Samantha thought nothing of running into my house to accuse me of wrongdoing without any evidence. It's fine with me if you *all* stay to hear the rest of what I have to say."

He connected with each person for a second before stabbing a finger in Sharon's direction. "You took me for a fool."

"Elias, that's not how—"

With his palm open toward her face, Elias said, "Spare me whatever rubbish you're going to spew. I've lived without knowing for thirty-two years. I'm sure I can do without you lying to me to get yourself out of this predicament."

Sighing, Michele said, "Papa, can you get to di point without all di theatrics?"

"The point is," Elias hissed, "Your uncle has Type A blood, and I give you one guess at *her* blood type."

Seething, although nausea rumbled in her stomach, Sam leapt to her feet and stood before Elias. "Father, that is so sick! You're telling me that because I'm the *wrong blood type*, that's enough reason for you to try to kill two people?"

Elias rose and stood at his full height, which was below Sam's eye level. "I'd say that's a damn good reason."

Her jaw trembled but she stiffened her spine. "Do you know that one of the men you sent to the hospital lost his life over this foolishness?"

"It may be foolishness to you, but to me, this is a betrayal. A disgraceful one." He threw a scathing look at Sharon as spittle flew from his mouth. "My wife and my brother. If I had my way, I'd shoot the two of them myself."

His vengeful words surged around Sam and ping-ponged in her head, leaving her unable to make sense of them. Her heart knew what they meant, though.

Ted stepped between them. "I don't care what you think you know. What *you've* done is disgraceful. I should—"

"You've done enough," Elias yelled and swung his fist.

The blow landed on Ted's chest, and he swung, hitting Elias on the cheek.

Enraged, Elias punched with both fists. His aim was off and he hit Sam twice in the face. Eyes gleaming with satisfaction, he said, "That's exactly what you deserve."

Sam's instinctive reaction was quick. Her hand swung back, then met her father's cheek. The blow stung and the imprint of her fingers on Elias' face brought Sam back into the room although her head swam. The second she regained her senses, they left again.

With his lips pulled back from his teeth, the man she'd called father all her life walloped her in the face a second time.

She jerked one arm up to protect her head as he gripped her hand hard, making her cry out. Elias squeezed tighter, then yelped and released Sam while he shook and shimmied on his feet. The watch had worked as intended, thanks to his merciless hold on her.

Sam crouched as a blur swept past.

The chair Elias had been using crashed on its side as Ted fell on top of him. Both men scrabbled on the floor with Ted's hands clasped around Elias' throat.

Michele and Sharon screamed and flailed their arms. The dogs yipped, but stayed out of the way of the men's thrashing feet. Sam was immune to the surreal scene playing out before her.

She had the sensation of standing in the middle of a hurricane with all the elements of nature at war. She couldn't separate one voice from another and only regained her sense of time and place when Kingston moved her out of the way then launched himself at both men. "Ted, let him go. You're going to kill him."

"That's what he deserves for hitting my daughter like that."

Yanking at the taller man, Kingston separated him from Elias, who lay wide-eyed and gasping on the tiles. He regained control of his breath and struggled to his feet, panting. Elias swayed, then stabilized himself by spreading his feet. In a hoarse whisper, he said, "Thank you for saving me from him and that little slut."

"This one's for them." Before anyone in the room could stop him, Kingston rammed his fist between Elias' eyes and left him sprawled on the floor, unconscious.

Chapter 26

"Are you sure it's okay to leave them alone to hash this out?" Hassan asked, leaning against the black Outlander. "I thought my family was full of what Americans call drama but the DaCostas are something else. More of an embarrassment for sure."

"They'll be fine for the next few minutes." Kingston clenched his jaw, then added, "If he's lucky, Elias will only need a few more minutes before he wakes up."

"For someone with such a calm personality, you went from zero to two hundred in a second," Ryan observed with a wry smile as he scanned the street, that ran below the level of the house.

Elias' heart condition barely created a blip on Kingston's conscience when *that* word slid out of his mouth, but he said, "Wouldn't you have done the same if someone tried that with your queen?"

"I can't argue with you there," Ryan said over his shoulder, as he walked down the driveway with the phone to his ear.

Kingston massaged the base of his skull, where a headache was in the making. He'd calmed down since the fisticuffs between Ted and Elias, if one could call it that.

In comparison to his folks, Sam's people were like firecrackers.

Kingston was beyond shocked at Elias' reaction after Sam returned his blows. No matter what she said or did, it was despicable to treat her that way, and to call her such a foul name. The man had allowed his hurt to turn into rage, which wasn't a good look. Normally, Kingston wasn't prone to open and unnecessary violence, but his reaction manifested itself before he stopped to think.

And to be honest, if the situation recurred, he'd do the same thing without regrets. Despite the reservations Sam harbored about their relationship because of her family, Kingston would defend her with his life. Murder wasn't off the table, either.

He turned toward the house, feeling the need to check on her. While she was a strong woman, Sam was on rocky ground after the revelation from her father.

Michele had rushed away and returned with two ice packs for Sam to use. The bruises had already formed on Sam's cheeks, even while she insisted everything was fine. She was sure to have a shiner, as well.

By now, Kingston hoped they had dealt with some of the skeletons from the past that had come tumbling out with such force. If what Elias said was true, their issues would take more than a minute to resolve.

He walked through the foyer and into the living room. All heads swiveled toward him and relief radiated from Sam's eyes. She stretched one hand in his direction while Michele and Ted stared at Kinston as though shell-shocked, and Sharon's gaze darted from one wall to the other.

Elias lay in a heap on the largest sofa with his mouth open and his eyes still closed. An angry welt, the size of Kingston's fist, marked his forehead.

Not that Elias deserved the courtesy, but Kingston hoped they had checked to see whether he was breathing.

Kingston sat next to Sam and pulled her to his chest. She let out a sigh, then said, "It's out in the open, Mom. So, you may as well tell me what happened."

"It wasn't the way Elias made it sound." Sharon twisted the wedding band on her finger while her shoulders sank. "Ted and I ..." She glanced at him before continuing, "We met at college and we ... later, I found out Pop had arranged for me to marry Elias, instead of Ted."

She scowled at Elias when he stirred and raised his head, then lay back on the seat staring at the ceiling as if he were alone.

The stillness grew oppressive and when it was clear no one would speak, Sharon said, "What we did was not intentional. I didn't know how to tell my father I was already in a relationship." She gestured with her chin to where Elias lay. "He went away for six months, which gave me time to end the affair with Ted. When Ted found out, he didn't wait around for me to explain that I wasn't playing around. I simply didn't know how to tell him that I had to do what my father wanted."

"Is that all it was to you? An affair?" Ted asked, turning from the window to sear Sharon with his eyes. "The long talks into the early mornings? We shared our future plans and none of that mattered?"

"You know it wasn't like that," she protested, spreading both hands. "I'm ashamed to admit that I didn't have the strength to fight for …" Her eyes widened as if she suddenly realized they weren't alone, and she sank in the seat, covering her face.

Next to her, Michele stared at Sam as though asking for an explanation which wasn't forthcoming.

All of it would have sounded preposterous to Kingston, if he didn't know his parents' history. His mother had seized the opportunity to teach abroad and escape her strict upbringing and her family's influence. The Changs would never have approved of her marrying a Black man, so she put herself out of their reach and did what satisfied her soul. By the time they found out she was legally wedded to Derrick Coburn, it was too late for them to do anything but disown her.

Although they'd been living in Montego Bay for a while after returning to Jamaica, a decade went by before the Changs reached out to JoAnne Coburn. By that time, she decided she was better off without them. Kingston had been in touch with his cousins for years, but never told his mother. This situation, though, was a whole other ball game.

"In all these years, it never once occurred to you that I'd want to know?" Ted asked, smoothing his ruffled hair. "That I had a right to know?"

"What was the point?" Sharon sniffled and dried her eyes with her sleeve. "It wasn't as if—"

Elias jackknifed into a sitting position. "She played us both for fools. Why would she want to give up her comfortable life when she had the best of both worlds?"

With a scornful expression, Sharon snapped, "As you well know, my family paid you a dowry, so don't act as if I came in rags and needing a place to say. If I had been stronger, I wouldn't have had to settle for you. Trust and believe, you are no prize, Elias DaCosta."

As if her tirade had used up all her strength, Sharon broke down in tears and shrank into the sofa, hugging a cushion.

"That's all well and good for you to say after the fact, but you're just a sl—"

"Don't you dare." Sam stood, trembling. "She's given you the best part of her life and all she's gotten from you are grief and misery." Sam clenched both fists as she delivered that accusation. "And the audacity to think you're better than anyone. You are exactly what everyone thinks—a cruel fool!"

"I don't expect anything else from you," Elias shot back as his attention shifted to Kingston. He tipped his chin in the air as if he'd smelled a noxious substance. "You are your mother's child, after all. No better herring, no better barrel."

"You're such an idiot. Stop right there." All movement ceased at Ted's commanding tone.

"What are you going to do?" Elias stood, then swayed before planting his feet.

When Ted moved toward his brother, Sam grabbed his arm. "Please stop. Whatever you're about to do isn't worth it. Let the law take care of him. He already has one murder to pay for."

Kingston was halfway to where they stood when the visual evidence of Elias' revelation struck him. Sam shared Ted's height, slender build, sandy blonde hair, deep-set hazel eyes, and full bottom lip. Their resemblance was now remarkable. What had been out in the open all this time now slammed him in the chest. Every word Elias spoke was true. Genetics was a funny thing, but no one in the DaCosta family was laughing.

Elias' protests snapped Kingston out of his thoughts.

"I will not be treated like a common criminal."

"That's not for you to decide," Ryan said, as he walked into the room. "The man you hired confessed to the police that you paid him to do what you couldn't do yourself. Someone lost their life doing your bidding. Those things will decide your fate. Three lives have been destroyed, not to mention the families. I promise, there will be nothing *common* about your situation."

Cackling, Elias said, "We all know that in this country, there's one law for the rich and another for the poor. I'm a member of the chamber of commerce and I sit on several boards, so—"

"None of that will help you in this particular case, Mr. DaCosta." The police officer who entered the room behind Ryan held up a folded sheet of paper as another uniformed officer moved toward Elias.

"This can't be happening," Elias snarled as his gaze darted between both policemen. "People like me don't—"

"Despite what you think, Mr. DaCosta, the law applies to *everyone*, even the delusional."

Elias stuck his chin in the air. "If you insist I must go with you, allow me to put on some proper clothing."

"Feel free to do so," the officer nodded. "We'll be waiting right here when you return."

With a fierce glare at Ted and Sharon, Elias sucked his teeth and marched out of their sight.

Chapter 27

"Why?" Ted's anguished question cut the tense atmosphere in the conference room.

They had landed in Chicago several days after the confrontation with Elias. The police had insisted they remain on the island, and sped up their investigation when Ted revealed he had to return to Chicago for an emergency meeting. They had done the required tests faced no issues coming through customs with their negative COVID-19 results.

Although Sam didn't think she had the capacity to deal with anything else, she insisted on being here this afternoon with Kingston to support Ted. She'd carefully applied makeup to cover the remaining bruises and avoided the searching gazes of the men, including Daron, while he opened Ted's phone and removed the doodad he'd installed.

The previous day, she had met with Khalil Germaine, mentor to the Kings and the conceptualizer behind The Castle. She'd been surprised to see him at such short notice, but had found him pleasant, charming, yet intense. Sam also realized where Jai, Vikkas, and their cousin had inherited their looks. Plus, that silver streak at his widow's peak that he'd passed on to Jai. Their conversation hadn't taken more than a half-hour and when it ended, Sam found that she'd been skillfully interviewed and given a passing grade. Khalil's promise that a confidential document would be sent for her signature and seal her induction as a Queen of the Castle brought deep satisfaction. Of course, Kingston deserved half the credit for what she'd uncovered.

Her focus returned to the horseshoe-shaped table, where Jai, Vikkas, Daron, Dro, Shaz, Hassan, and Ryan were seated. Their mentor was not part of these proceedings.

Nicco and Angela stood outside the door.

Ted's lifelong friend, Bronson Hardy, stared at him across the polished expanse of wood with his mouth twisted in a smirk. "Where should I begin?"

Dressed in dark trousers and a wrinkled blue short-sleeved shirt, he didn't look like the savvy businessman he was touted to be by the newspapers. His face was lined and haggard, as if he needed sleep, which was understandable since he'd been denied the luxury of a bed for some time.

"Start wherever it pleases you." Ted sighed. "At this point, another few blows won't make a difference."

The men around them watched and listened, but no one intervened. Hardy had been released by the police an hour ago. Even though humbled by spending hours in lockup, defiance radiated from him.

Earlier, Nicco and Angela had replaced his designated driver, corralled him inside an SUV identical to his own, and swept him to The Castle. By the time he realized what was happening, Hardy could do nothing about the situation. Daron's equipment had jammed any calls he tried to make from the back of the vehicle and Angela had gently warned him that if he made any sudden and unwelcome moves, she'd put him in the hospital, or the morgue. Her threat kept him subdued until they arrived at The Castle.

"You see, it's like this." Hardy glowered and laid his large fists on the wooden surface of the table. His dark eyes matched his deep-mahogany complexion. "You always had everything. When the opportunity came for MiVaxx to expand their research capacity, I knew you'd be the perfect candidate to buy in because you'd have the money." A couple of seconds passed before he added, "It's always been that way."

Ted shook his head as if confused. "So what? You've worked hard and now own several businesses. You have investments and the best of everything."

"But *you're* the one who's a member of The Castle," Hardy snapped. "You didn't have to cash in any of your investments or break into your savings to come up with the money to invest in MiVaxx. Ted, you always had it easy."

Ted massaged his temples and squinted at Hardy. "We've been friends since high school. You've been in my home many times with my family—"

"Who barely tolerated me because my skin didn't look like yours." He sneered, then folded his arms. "Didn't you ever wonder why it was that whenever I visited your house we had to eat in the kitchen? And I was only allowed in the living room when I was headed through the front door?"

When Ted frowned, Hardy continued, "Of course not, you were so comfortable with who you were, it didn't occur to you that your family treated me like something you'd dragged home from one of the school dumpsters."

"But *I* never considered you as anything other than my best friend." Staring him in the eyes, Ted asked, "So all this time, you've hated me? Yet you stuck to me as if you didn't have all this bitterness inside you?"

Hardy shrugged and gave him a sour look. "You do what you must to survive. Your friendship and family influence in Jamaica opened doors that would have been slammed shut in my face if I weren't connected to you."

Ted's hands shook when he spread them on the table. "So, this abduction you arranged. Was that really meant for you or for me? And that ruse to expose the MiVaxx side effects also came from you, but you miscalculated whoever you were using. Probably didn't pay them what you promised and they released the story anyway."

"Who told you that?" Hardy's head reared back and a vein throbbed in his temple. "The problem with you is that you're stubborn and refuse to part with your money."

"And the problem with you is making an assumption that I've had everything handed to me on a golden platter. I've worked hard to add to what my family provided." Ted stabbed a finger in Hardy's direction. "You know that better than anyone. Envy doesn't look good on you, Bronson."

Vikkas studied both men with his fingers steepled under his chin. Ryan and Kingston exchanged a knowing look.

"If you had just given up the money, that story wouldn't have been released," Hardy hissed through clenched teeth.

"Now, tell me why I'd have done that." Ted released a dry chuckle. "Fact is, when you treat people well, they have no need to play a game of double-cross, but you wouldn't know that."

He rested against the back of the chair and drummed on the table. "Imagine my surprise when I touched down in Jamaica and received a text to say I could *save myself some embarrassment* if I paid more than you were paying to suppress that story. Or should I say, more than you gave them to threaten me with exposure, knowing very well I was not aware of the half of what that drug was doing to people."

"Since I didn't know the backstory on the drug, I hedged my bets." He tapped the table again. "Held my ground until I had better information. Come to find out, you arranged that kidnapping. And if you did that, what else wouldn't you do? Seems I was right."

Sam exchanged a glance with Kingston, who suppressed a smile. She wondered how he could find the situation amusing. But when she thought about it, her uncle … or rather, her father would be considered a force to come up against based on his quiet resistance. Except for the parts where he gave them anxious moments by keeping his silence. Kingston was like that, too. Their discussion about his trip had been tossed to the side, admittedly through no fault of his. Time hadn't allowed it.

But up to the present time, he hadn't said a word about the article she was now certain he was writing. She'd peeked at his screen yesterday evening and confirmed what she suspected. The disappointment made her stomach plummet and she absorbed the pain and shrugged off his attempts to find out what had affected her mood. "I'm just blue about what happened in Jamaica," she'd said.

They couldn't move forward without clearing the air between them.

Not with the resentment she was carrying. What he'd done was to steal her story idea. The most worrisome issue was that Kingston could write rings around her. They both knew it. He had a way with language and could unknot the most troublesome string of words and weave them into clear and potent sentences. In the past, he'd used that skill to help her. Now, he was competing with her.

She glanced at him, and he flashed her a smile that warmed her heart even after everything she'd been thinking.

Ted's voice brought back the present.

"There's something I'd still like to know. It's one thing to have a grudge against me, who you know almost as well as yourself, but what did those people taking this poison drug ever do to you? To the company?"

"Oh please, Ted, you were always such a sympathizer to the under-dog." Hardy shook his head. "There's no malice involved. It's all about business. The company invested too much in studying the Ebzirton vac-cine to admit failure after so many years of investing money in it. How would it look to the public if we had come out and said the drug didn't work the way it was intended? The company and all of its investors would have been ruined."

Jai's face grew stormy as he asked, "What about adjusting your sails, changing the make-up of the chemicals, doing more clinical stud-ies. Just trying something different to get better results?"

"You don't get it," Hardy ground out while clenching his jaws. "Mi-Vaxx invested too much money to start over or change course."

"So instead, you all conspired to ruin the lives of poor people," Jai said with heat in his gaze.

Hardy wore a blank expression and spoke in a matter-of-fact tone. "As long as there are poor and underprivileged people in the world, someone will take advantage. It's just the way things work."

"Not on my watch," Jai said, sliding a pad and pen to Hardy. "I'm going to need the name of all the directors who are in on this, and opted to do nothing."

"That would be everyone." Hardy's gaze went to Ted.

"You don't understand," Jai said, with both brows pulled low over his eyes. "I need the names of those who had inside information. Those who knew and endorsed poisoning those people to make a profit."

"What am I getting out of it?" Hardy asked.

"The chance to do something decent, for once in your life, and make restitution." Vikkas lowered his chin and tipped one brow, which Sam took to mean Hardy should be satisfied.

"Or the chance to keep breathing," Dro said, and a chilly silence descended over the room.

"Agreed." Shaz dropped his pen on the pad where he'd been making notes. "A few years off the forty-year sentence staring you in the face is better than nothing. Think about the thousands of people whose lives you've helped to destroy."

"Who says I'm going to prison?" Hardy scanned the people around him as if only now aware of the predicament facing him.

"You're a bright man, Bronson," Ted said. "Figure it out."

"I'm not taking the heat for this alone. I'm not any of the scientists or the people at the top of this food chain."

"But you aided and abetted the process," Shaz said, twirling his pen. "That puts you high up and you know about that proverb that says the higher a monkey climbs—"

"The more his bottom is exposed," Hassan said.

"It doesn't quite go like that"—Ryan quipped, then smiled at Sam—"but since we're in polite company …"

"And since you're from Durabia," Daron said, picking up his tablet. "What would you know about that?"

"I'm more than just the King of Durabia's nephew, and a Knight assigned to help with this case." Hassan wore a sly expression as he continued, "I've been hanging out with Ryan. He taught me a thing or three."

Daron's amused expression vanished when his attention moved back to Hardy, who frowned as his focus shifted to the pen and paper. Letting out a resigned sigh, he pulled them toward him.

"That's the right choice," Ted said, with regret clouding his eyes. "It's ironic that you've ruined your life over making money when you have so much of it already."

"Here's the thing." Vikkas sat back from the table. "Those who don't have money will never understand the struggles those who do have it go through to keep what they have and earn even more of it. That's where some of us lose our way."

"You've got that right." As Sam rested a hand on his thigh, Kingston continued, "The worst stories I've covered have to do with those who had the power to make a difference but didn't because profit was more important than philanthropy."

Hardy's gaze flicked to Kingston, but he didn't comment.

"I'm grateful some good will come out of all this," Sam murmured. "Lives will be saved."

"That's right. And some people will be compensated." Leaning closer, he added, "I hope you're close to the end of your story. It's going to be your best yet, not to mention explosive."

The compliment should have made her ecstatic, instead it dampened her mood. She had to slay this dragon before it ate her alive.

Chapter 28

"I feel like a scratched disk," Kingston said, rolling his head toward her. "In the past month, it's like I've been asking you what's wrong all the time. Will you talk to me, woman?"

"Since you asked …" Sam swung sideways on the seat to face him. The movement dislodged his hand from her hair. "I do need to chat with you."

"Sounds serious." He sat up and lowered the sound on the television. After the meeting with the Kings, they had returned upstairs where they ordered dinner. Ted had gone out for the evening, so they had the suite to themselves.

"It is. But first, I wanted you to know that my position as a Queen of the Castle will soon become official."

"That's wonderful." He grinned and patted her leg. "I suppose that came about partly as a result of breaking open the story. Good job, lady."

"The best part is that the role puts me in a position to do some good work under the auspices of The Castle." She smiled, but didn't seem happy. "Ted's membership gave me the edge I didn't know I needed."

Kingston tapped her chin. "Like I said, well done. You so deserve this."

"Thank you." After pulling one side of her lip into her mouth, Sam met his gaze with troubled eyes. "I know what you're doing."

Both her words and reaction confused him. "Huh?"

"I know about the article you're writing." She released a heavy breath as if she was carrying an unbearable burden, then said, "And I'm wondering how you could do that to me … after everything."

"Wait. What? I remember you mentioned something to that effect while we were in Jamaica, but with everything else, it got pushed to the side." He put a hand to his chest where his heart thumped with deep, painful beats. "Let me get this straight. You're accusing me of trying to steal your thunder?"

"I wouldn't put it like that——"

"But it's what you mean." His frown deepened while he rubbed the stubble on his jaw. "And it's exactly what you're saying."

"Because that's what it looks like to me," she insisted as her gaze skimmed the elegant suite.

He smiled, but it wasn't a genuine gesture. "Exactly what evidence are you working with, Samantha?"

Cocking one brow, she pulled back. "So, we're all formal and everything now that I found out what you did?"

"I didn't *do* anything." He spread both hands. "But since you're so sure I *did* something, feel free to show me the proof."

Sam's eyes darkened and she played with the diamond pendant on the gold chain around her neck as if suddenly unsure of herself. When he continued staring at her, she pointed at the center table.

"Open your iPad."

He picked it up and brought the screen to life. Then he handed it to her, folded both arms, and leaned back. "Show me."

Eyes narrowed, she scanned the files. Then she tapped a couple of times and handed him the tablet. "That's what I'm talking about … *Kingston.*"

A glance told him what file she'd looked at and why Sam was accusing him, but his stomach sank. An invisible band tightened across his chest and disappointment filled his belly. Now, the reason for her unexplained mood swings became clear. The way she looked at him while talking to Trey-Jon and Evita as he was taking notes. The things she said … *Does it have to do with that article you're writing? Don't act like you don't know what I'm talking about. It seems to me that you're putting together the same story—*"

She had tried to spit out her accusations, but he'd been too busy with Ted's business to understand what she meant. Kingston laid the iPad on the seat between them and allowed his mind to settle. If he went with his first words, Sam might not speak to him again. Ever.

"Didn't you wonder why I'd continue to keep it open if I had anything to hide?"

Her focus shifted to the television and she shrugged. "You're used to leaving it that way, so—"

"So what, Sam? I forgot and left it open because I was trying to do *what* again?" He tapped his forehead, where a headache was brewing. "Ah, yes, steal your story from under you."

She shoved both hands through her hair. "It looked like you were writing the same thing."

"But from a different angle." He clicked his tongue against his teeth. "You were so willing to believe the worst of me, you didn't look further than what you were convinced I was doing."

"Why were you writing it anyway?" Her tone was defiant, but less confident than a moment ago.

"There is no copyright on ideas or stories." He reached for the iPad and swiped the screen, navigated to the bottom, and stopped at the by-line. "Here."

Seconds after her gaze landed on the tablet, it shot to him. Her fingers moved quickly across the screen, but he didn't ask what she was doing. When her attention returned to him, Sam pursed her lips to stop them from trembling as her eyes turned glossy. "Kingston," she whispered.

"Next time, think twice, or follow through and clarify what I'm doing before you decide I'm stealing." She opened her mouth, but he held up one hand. "This is the worst thing you could have accused me of doing. We both know my views on personal integrity."

Gently, he eased the tablet from Sam's fingers, scooped his keys off the table, and stood.

"You're leaving?" she asked, blinking several times.

He rubbed the back of his neck, suddenly weary. "I'm gonna call it a night."

Sam trailed him to the door and when he stood on the other side, she gripped his shirtsleeve. "Kingston, let's talk about this."

"The time for that was when you first suspected I was up to no good."

She lowered her chin, but locked gazes with him. "You're right, and I'm—"

"Yeah, I know." His lips puckered and he scoffed. "You're sorry."

Instead of releasing him, Sam kissed him and nudged his mouth open with her tongue. The connection was electric and made him forget everything that had happened in the past few minutes. Until he raised his head and good sense returned. He stepped out of her reach. "I *suspect* we might talk later."

Some of her spark returned and she pulled back her shoulders, even as her eyes sparkled. "Don't say that if you don't mean it. Saying you *suspect* doesn't give me much hope."

"You're right, but I need some time to think." He touched her cheek, then backed away from the door. "The fact is, if we don't have trust, we have nothing."

***

One week later, Samantha still didn't know how to repair the damage she'd done. She'd spoken with Kingston several times, but he flew back to New York before she did. Pride and confusion kept her from forcing a face-to-face encounter.

While she'd written about the humanitarian contributions of The Castle, Kingston's article centered around the people that made up The

Castle. Aside from the Kings she'd met, plus several others she had yet to meet—including Grant, Mariano, Kaleb, and Dwayne—he featured the women and Queens. Dr. Lani Jamison, Bobbi Raye Bennett, Solange Porter, Luiza Eituk, Caressa Sidaná, Milan Jackson, Cassandra Toussaint, and Pilar Silva were proudly making an impact around the world, where others had failed.

She'd emailed the article to herself and when she finished reading the thorough and thought-provoking piece Kingston wrote, she knew the Queens better than she had before. His professionalism was unquestioned, but the thing that pierced her heart and made her want to weep was the byline. Kingston had included both their names and made a notation.

Discuss with Sam - collaborate/complete when we land in Chicago/ New York.

Two days earlier, she returned to New York without a plan. She was still dealing with her father's betrayal and getting used to Ted's role as a father, rather than an uncle. The fallout from Elias' actions had brought their family's name down to gutter level and made her remorseful over what Michele and Mom had to deal with since the story broke. A twinge of guilt mingled with relief that she wasn't living through the aftermath in Jamaica, but an echo of embarrassment rang through her as she knocked on Kingston's door.

When he opened it, she searched his face and eyes, which were expressionless. She'd have her work cut out for her.

Kingston was the same, yet different. He was more watchful. Cautious even. In a glance, she absorbed his polo shirt, sweatpants, and bare feet.

Without conscious thought, she cupped his jaw and let her fingers trail over the beginnings of a beard. "Since I broke what we had, I've come to see if you will give me the chance to fix it."

He stepped away from the door and let her into his apartment.

Sam hadn't realized how much she missed the sound of his voice. While they'd had several stilted conversations on the phone, she longed to hear his low, sexy, unhurried speech close to her ear.

The second-floor Washington Heights apartment was as immaculate as the last time she'd been inside it. The sectional sofa sat opposite the shelving that housed Kingston's stereo and collection of books. In one corner, a long-neck floor lamp arched over a potted palm and a sturdy coffee table.

At his invitation, she chose a seat at the small end of the gray sofa and laid down her bag.

"Want something to drink?" he asked.

"No, sit with me." She touched the cushion. "Please."

Kingston moved his iPad to the coffee table and did as she asked.

In the silence surrounding them, she didn't know where else to focus her attention, so she fixed her eyes on the window overlooking the street. When he didn't break the silence, Sam bolstered her courage and forgot about the rehearsed words that had scattered in seven directions at the sight of him.

"I don't have a pretty speech prepared." She smoothed her hair, then decided not to lie. "Actually, I did, but it disappeared the moment I looked at you."

One side of his mouth curved in a lopsided smile. "You know that's corny right?"

"Mmm-hmm." She studied her hands, then stared at the ceiling. "I've had time to think. I should have trusted you, especially since you've never given me a reason not to. When I thought about all the work I'd put into the article and the possibility of coming away with a story that wouldn't hit as hard, I guess I—"

"Lost your mind?"

She looked directly at him, wanting to clap back but now wasn't the time. "I guess."

Kingston stared deep into her eyes. "What I can't figure out is why you believe I'd compete with you … betray you … steal from you … yet sleep with you."

"Haven't you ever made a mistake?" she asked. Sam despised the pleading note in her voice, but wanted her man back. "Reached a conclusion that later turned out to be wrong?"

He released a sign as he massaged his chin. "Of course, but babe, sometimes you should slow down, assess the material in front of you, ask some questions, and *then* do what you have to do. Instead, you go off half-cocked, which never helps any situation."

"I've admitted I was wrong several times. Can't you find it in your heart to forgive me?"

"Sam, it's not about that. I forgave you the moment you asked. This habit you have of accusing first and then waiting for an explanation later will get you in serious trouble one day."

She wanted to move past the recriminations and get to the heart of why she'd come, but Kingston wasn't making it easy. After racking her brain and not finding a way around the roadblock, she sank against the sofa. Finally, she said, "I miss you, Kingston and I need us. I want you back."

He rose and moved to the window to stare at the street. When the tension became too much, Sam crossed the room, and wrapped her arms around him. But he didn't budge or acknowledge her. Eyes closed, she inhaled his scent. A moment later, she left him and picked up her handbag off the sofa. She opened it and left a paper bag on the center table. For now, she'd give Kingston the space he needed, but didn't intend to lose him. That wasn't part of her plan. She needed this man the way she needed air. He was everything to her and she'd make sure he knew it.

When she was at the door, Sam looked over her shoulder. Kingston now stood next to the center table with her gift in hand.

"So, you came over here to bribe me with a bag full of grater cake?" He crushed the mouth of the paper bag closed and set it down. When he stood straight, Kingston shook his head. "What kind of man do you think I am? One who can be bought with stuff I like that's not good for me?"

His gentle smile restored her balance and as she searched his eyes, Sam's assurance grew.

"That's not what I think at all." Taking a few steps closer, she said, "You're the man I love, cherish, and respect. And because of that, I also know you wouldn't object to me bringing you a little something to help smooth a rough patch."

They stared at each other for an eternity. Much was conveyed, but no words were spoken. Another age went by before he opened his arms. "Sam, get over here and gimme some love."

Chapter 29

"Wait, wait!" Michele's voice carried through Sam's cell phone to Kingston, where he sat in the driver's seat. They were approaching his parents' house, located in Hudson, a small city on the outskirts of New York. Since their retirement, Derrick and JoAnne preferred the slower pace to the hectic life in New York City.

He glanced across at Sam when she let out a peal of laughter. "Grandma Esmie will be the death of me. She told me to make sure I didn't come back without a few additional pounds and some good news for her."

A sober expression came to her face, then she said, "I know, but you can manage. If there's a way to stay out of prison, I don't doubt he'll find it. Being out on bail will give him enough time to figure out whose arm he can twist. He can certainly afford the best lawyers."

She paused, then continued in a reflective way, "I don't see any kind of reconciliation on the horizon. Let's just say, Elias DaCosta isn't on my list of priorities right now."

After a few seconds of silence, she said, "I'm sure Grandma Esmie will enjoy the company. That's if Mom doesn't start getting in her way. I'll call Mom later today."

Sam dropped the phone in her bag and leaned toward him. "Almost there?"

"In another couple of minutes."

She inhaled deeply but didn't say more. Instead, she stared out the window.

"Stop worrying. Everything will work out fine."

"Yes, it always does. We just need to let things take their natural course." She swiped the hair away from her face and that's when he noticed she wasn't wearing the ring he gave her.

Two weeks ago, she flew back to New York. After their reconciliation, they worked on Sam's story, which she formally invited him to co-author. They combined what they each wrote and emerged with a stronger and more detailed feature.

The article—heralded by Catherine as "Pulitzer Prize worthy"—detailing the pharmaceutical cover-up and the resulting effects in several African countries had been the leading item in the newspaper on Monday of this week. Just as Kingston predicted, their research and writing made such a huge impact, they had been invited to do several interviews on television news magazine programs. They also received offers to fund writing and research on several other aspects of the healthcare industry.

With the bonus they received from the article, and donations from business people Sam contacted locally, they started a foundation in Jamaica. All the money they made would be used to educate a select number of children, whose parents had lost their lives to gun violence.

"Have you thanked Trey-Jon for helping you to break this story?" Sam asked when they had wrapped up their writing by sharing a bottle of port wine on Kingston's sofa.

"Wouldn't hear the end of it if I didn't," he said before sipping from his glass.

"Did you ask if he and Evita made contact?" she asked, looking up at him.

"You're late. They've spoken twice since our teleconference."

With a dreamy smile, she said, "Let's hope they finally make something of this."

He eased closer and dropped one arm around Sam. "If it's meant to be, it will happen."

Clinking their glasses together, Sam nodded. "I like the way you think."

Kingston's thoughts went back to the MiVaxx exposé. Even in putting the pieces of their story together, he had enjoyed every minute with Sam and was satisfied by their joint effort. He'd even linked with his friend Max again for information to help Sam complete her feature on an outstanding teenager with autism, and had proofed the finished product. In turn, she discussed ways in which he could use his contacts to write his China story without leaving her side.

MiVaxx was currently under investigation by the FDA, with several board members facing charges. Others had resigned and already lawsuits were being filed against the company. Hardy had been arrested and released on bail, pending the completion of the investigation.

"Hey," Kingston asked, "Have you heard from Ted lately?"

"I know what you're trying to do." She grinned but didn't turn her head.

"I'd ask if it's working but I already know the answer."

Ted had jetted off to the Bahamas for a week, declaring that he needed to declutter his brain. Of course, that was after he celebrated Sam's new status at The Castle.

Sam rubbed his chin and giggled. "He's enjoying the slow pace of life and reevaluating, he says."

Ever since the shooting on the Martha Brae River, Kingston had been thinking about what life would be like without Sam in it. While they feverishly completed their research and decided what to keep and eliminate, his mind had churned in the background. By the time they refined and closed the exposé, Kingston concluded he didn't want to do life without her.

Last night, after an evening spent wining and dining her, which Sam thought was intended to celebrate the success of their story, Kingston took her home. He knew how much Sam enjoyed Devon House ice cream, a specialty treat sold at a local historical landmark with the same name.

He'd managed to get it to the States with them, agonizing all the way that it would have been a messy puddle by the time they returned. But he'd been very lucky the Devon stout—that imitated the flavor of the Jamaican malt beer Dragon stout—was soft but salvageable. He stored it in the back of the freezer and waited for the right moment.

Kingston shared Sam's ice cream, watching to be sure she didn't accidentally ingest a mouthful of 24-karat gold. Her reaction when the spoon hit the ring in the bottom of the bowl was priceless. Sam blinked a couple of times as if she didn't understand what she was seeing. She lifted the ring onto the spoon and studied it as if she'd never seen one in her life. Then her eyes darkened and swam with tears.

Sniffing, she asked, "Can't you do ordinary stuff, like other people?"

He shook his head and didn't waste time with pretty language, although she deserved all of it. Kingston knew his end goal and wanted it now. "Samantha DaCosta, will you be my everything? Accept my love, take my name, bear my children, be part of my forever?"

When she let out a heavy breath but didn't answer, he waited for Sam to process his proposal. Her silence lasted for a while, so he gave her space to think. The same way he did while she absorbed the fact that Ted was her biological father. He had given her space to work through her emotions and listened when she poured out her feelings over everything her family revealed in Jamaica. By the time he washed the bowl, spoon, and ring, Sam had found the words she needed.

He took his place next to her and waited while she climbed into his lap and settled with her head against his chest. She slid both arms around his neck, kissed his chin, and sighed. "I love you more than I can find words to tell you. Yes, I'll be your wife."

With both arms cinched tight around her waist, Kingston softly kissed her lips. "Good, 'cause I was about to tell your father that you weren't acting right."

Sam pulled her head back and frowned. "Say what?"

He kissed her again. "I didn't tell you which father, did I? But for your information, I asked Ted for your hand."

Grinning, she said, "Look at you sounding old-fashioned and what-not."

"I may be hip and all, but I believe in doing things the proper way, especially when they concern you."

Chapter 30

Now that they sat outside his parents' house, Kingston sensed Sam's apprehension. The first meeting between Sam and his parents at a restaurant had been stiff and uncomfortable because Mom and Dad had issues.

JoAnne Coburn wanted to choose a suitable female for Kingston, while Derrick Coburn would have preferred seeing him with someone of his race. Since Kingston knew he couldn't please either of them where their preferences were concerned, he'd never tried. He simply made choices that served him well. His relationship with Sam was no different.

He went around to the passenger side of the Honda CR-V to assist Sam. By the time they climbed the steps, his father and mother emerged on the small veranda of their three-bedroom home. A small, personable woman who wore her jet-black hair in a neat bun, his mother stretched to kiss his cheek. Her dark eyes sparkled in her round face. "I can't believe it's been a month since I last saw you."

"Time waits for no man, as you'd say, Mom."

"That's right," she said, laughing. Her smile dimmed a little when she greeted Sam. "Thanks for coming. It's good to see you again."

"Same here." Sam put out both hands and to Kingston's surprise, his mother embraced her.

After enfolding him in a bear hug, Derrick Coburn gave Sam a side hug. "Welcome," he said. "Let's go around the back."

They went through the house which was roomy, yet cozy. A giant oriental fan decorated one wall and several strategically placed urns with dried flowers drew the eyes. They emerged on the back patio, which gave them a great view of the river.

His father, a tall, brawny man with a full beard, gestured toward the water. "I'm sure you'll appreciate the view.

"This is spectacular," Sam exclaimed on catching sight of the panoramic spread before them. "And your home is lovely. The Oriental theme reminds me of Jamaica."

"Really?" JoAnne asked with a smile. "I welcome your comments on the similarities."

Sam returned the gesture, then said, "I'm familiar with several Chinese families. Besides the popularity of the name "Chin," they have beautiful homes and restaurants that are big on oriental themes. A taste of China in Jamaica, you could say."

JoAnne covered her mouth to keep the sound of her laughter between the two. "Oh my goodness. I thought you were going with the old joke, "Jamaica has more Chins than a Chinese phone book.""

"That was going to be on my next visit." Sam turned her gaze back to the water. "At least, I hope there will be another one."

"I would be very upset if you didn't return. We enjoy it here because it's quiet and beautiful," JoAnne said after following the direction in which Sam was focused. "Have a seat when you're ready."

Still gazing at the horizon, Sam nodded. "Thank you, I will."

They had not eaten before leaving Kingston's apartment, based on his mother's instructions, so he wolfed down a delicious and filling lunch of curried goat with basmati rice and raw vegetables.

When JoAnne mentioned that she'd prepared sweet potato pudding for dessert, Kingston groaned. "You should have told me this before I ate everything."

"Not to worry." Sam patted his arm. "I'll have your share. I love sweet potato pudding."

Chuckling, his father said, "For a slender woman, I like the way you eat."

Sweeping her hair out of the way, Sam grinned. "You do remember that I'm Jamaican, right?"

JoAnne nodded as she said, "That was a surprise when we first met, and a bit of a relief really."

Her comment surprised Kingston because she'd been reserved up to now. Also, her reaction *that* time did not convey relief, but carried veiled hostility. The telephone conversation on Thursday primed them for this visit. In a few words, he shared that he expected them to pay Sam the courtesy she deserved.

Kingston took Sam's hand in his, stroking the back of it with his thumb. "Mom, Dad, I've asked Sam to be my wife, and she said yes."

A few seconds of silence hung over the patio. Even the breeze seemed non-existent. Then a smile broke over his dad's face. "Congratulations to the two of you."

His mother's response was more muted, when she said, "You have my son's heart. If you take care of his, you'll have mine."

"Thanks, ma'am. We'll take good care of each other."

"And one other thing," JoAnne stood, and a smile replaced the caution she'd exuded. She walked around the table to where Sam was seated and gripped one of her hands. "When you visit again, I expect you to wear a lovely Kimono because I'm planning a traditional Chinese feast."

Sam laid a hand on her chest. "I'm sorry, I don't have one and I've never worn one before."

"Oh my dear, of course, you have a beautiful Kimono." JoAnne picked up a box off a nearby chair. "There's also a San."

"A San?"

"Yes, a San is a Chinese umbrella. You must remember that it will protect and cover you from the rain, but it will not keep rain from falling. In your life expect rain. It will nourish or flood you with pesky storm clouds. How you handle it is up to you and my son."

JoAnne raised one hand to keep Sam from standing. "I'm not finished."

"I'm sorry." She leaned forward waiting for JoAnne to complete her thoughts.

"Now that we've had a chance to talk, I see something special in you. One who has untapped knowledge and strength; one such as a Queen." She pointed to Kingston and winked. "Of course, it is as it should be. You are about to marry a king." She bowed slightly and added, "Of course, I've heard about The Castle, too."

Sam glanced at Kingston, who only smiled. She hadn't revealed the details of her contractual arrangements as a Queen of the Castle, but he was aware that she'd received an envelope containing documents, which she'd signed and returned to Vikkas. All without any fanfare or detailed explanation, and he respected that.

"You need not say anything. Your future blabbermouth husband told me about your adventures and gave me your size a week ago. I can't wait to see you in it, you'll look gorgeous. How could you not? You did say I had exquisite taste."

Chuckling, Sam rose and hugged his mother tight enough to shave two inches off her five-foot frame.

"Blabbermouth? Really, mother." He raised both eyebrows. "You were the one who—"

"Be respectful, my son, before I cancel your birth certificate and the upcoming wedding."

Angling his body toward his father, Kingston said, "Dad, you're not going to help your one and only son with these women ganging up on me?"

"Nope, you're on your own. But I do have a concern."

"What concern?" Kingston sipped from his glass, then asked, "What did I do wrong?"

"Is this how you young'uns are doing it these days?" Derrick Coburn asked, tugging gently at his beard.

"What d'you mean?" Kingston said, as a gentle wind blew across the patio.

"In my day, when we asked a woman for her hand, a ring was involved."

Sam went beet red before she said, "He gave me a beautiful one, but I left it at home."

"Be sure you're wearing it the next time I see you." Derrick's gaze shifted to Kingston. "Otherwise, there's no telling who might walk away with your woman."

"Agreed." Sam and Kingston spoke at the same time, then chuckled.

Kingston's gaze went to his mother. "So about that potato pudding …"

"Didn't you say you were full?" JoAnne asked.

"You know what?" Kingston eased out of his chair and helped Sam to stand. "Let's go for a walk. The pudding will be our reward when we return."

"I like the sound of that," she said.

Hand in hand, they went down the sidewalk, enjoying the greenery and the blue waters of the river. Twenty feet from the bank, Kingston dropped one arm around her shoulder and spoke into her ear. "Why did you leave the ring?"

She avoided his eyes, staring straight ahead. "I kinda felt like an impostor, so I left it behind."

"Hoping I wouldn't tell them today, right?"

"Something like that," she answered but didn't turn her head, as if spellbound by the water.

"It doesn't matter what my parents think about you, Sam. You're marrying me, not my mom and dad."

"I understand that, but in case you weren't planning on letting them know now, there wouldn't be any awkwardness. But, the visit was nothing like I imagined and I'm grateful for that."

"Come here, you." Kingston wrapped both arms around Sam and

dropped kisses all over her face and neck. He avoided applying pressure to the diamond studs she now wore that could summon a team of powerful men, if they thought she was in any kind of danger. "It's been quite a journey to this point and I look forward to life with you."

She rubbed his back under his thin sweater, finally looking him in the eyes. "Never doubt that I love you. By refusing to commit to you, I was taking the coward's way out. I didn't want the struggle of fighting my family, plus whatever people would say about us. We already know what that's like."

"And now?" he asked, nuzzling her neck.

"At this point, I don't give a rat's behind anymore. I want to be with you, take care of you, love on you, and everything else our life together has to offer."

While lifting her chin so their eyes connected, Kingston whispered, "As long as I'm alive, you'll be the queen of my heart."

"And you'll always be my king," she replied, then sealed their lips in a sizzling kiss filled with promises for the future.

When he raised his head, she said, "However, if you gave your mother the wrong size for that Kimono, your kingdom may collapse."

"Never," he said, nipping the side of her neck. "This king knows what's good for him."

About the Authors

National Bestselling Author, J.L. Campbell writes contemporary, paranormal, and sweet romance, romantic suspense, inspirational and women's fiction, as well as new and young adult novels. Campbell, who hails from Jamaica, has penned more than forty books.

She is a certified editor, and book coach. When she's not writing, Campbell adds to her extensive collection of photos detailing Jamaica's flora and fauna. Visit her on the web at amazon.com/author/jlcampbell or www.joylcampbell.com

Connect with her on social media via Sociatap. https://sociatap.com/JL_Campbell

Pat G'Orge-Walker is the Essence, and National bestselling and award-winning author of the Christian fiction Sister Betty comedy series, as well as contemporary fiction, Women's issues, Romance novels. The novels published by Kensington/Dafina that fearlessly burrow into issues sometimes labeled taboo or left unsaid by Christian and secular community without subverting the Good News or watering down the potency of its message. She is also a contributor to New York Times anthologies and a three-time AALAS winner for Comedy as well as several other prestigious awards. Pat, a PK, has quietly soaked up material from her father's Baptist congregation and her mother's Pentecostal assembly to create and keep her audiences howling with laughter, performing nationwide and on the high seas with her One-Woman comedy show, "Sister Betty! God's Calling You!"

Before entering the Publishing arena, she was a recording industry veteran working promotion/marketing with Epic, Columbia and Def Jam records. And, before that, she sang with Arlene Smith and the Chantels (Maybe, He's Gone, Look in My Eyes.)

Today, she is constantly looking to connect further with her reader and fan base. www.pgorgewalker.com as The First Lady of Gospel Comedy forges a successful

career as author and comedian. She currently resides in NC.

Find her on the web and social media:

https://sociatap.com/sisterbetty/

Facebook Author page – https://www.facebook.com/sisterbetty

Instagram – https://bit.ly/patgorgewalkeronInstagram

Amazon Author Page –

Twitter – https://bit.ly/pgorgewalkerontwitter

Pat G'Orge-Walker – www.pgorgewalker.com

KING OF EVANSTON

"Why do you think she's going to kill him?"

Shaz turned away from the group of teenagers, who were using barbells and didn't need to be distracted. He waited for her answer as his stomach twisted. Camilla Gibson was going to give him a heart attack in no time with her reckless antics.

As he concentrated on the caller, he dabbed his forehead with the towel hanging around his neck.

"Camilla is on her way to Alderman Bennett's office," Miss Mabel whispered.

"After I told her specifically not to do that." With his free hand, Shaz motioned to the boys. "Continue with your reps. I'll be right back."

The clanging of metal from various gym equipment filled the air as the young men followed his instruction. He stalked to the plate glass door, absently wiping away sweat that poured from his skin. When he addressed Miss Mabel, the owner of the Jamaican restaurant where he ate regularly, he lowered his voice. "I'm in the middle of a workout with the boys and I'm scheduled to have a session with them after—"

"I know they're important," Miss Mabel said, her accent growing deeper as her pitch climbed. "But dis is urgent, too. If ya don' come, I might have to kill ya."

"Why would you want to do that?" he asked, biting back a chuckle. Miss Mabel was always high drama, same as her niece.

"Because my sister might fly over from Jamaica and kill me after Camilla get herself in trouble."

Staring at the red brick building across the street, he said, "You mean more than she's in already?"

"Boy, don't joke at a time like dis." Miss Mabel's voice took on a desperate edge. "Ya comin' or not?"

Despite the way his gut twisted, an involuntary grin lifted his lips as he pictured her scowling. "Don't worry. I'll meet you there in fifteen minutes."

"Ya better make dat ten. The way dat gal behavin', she might be packin'."

The thought chilled his blood.

Camilla, Miss Mabel's niece, was in the U.S. accessing treatment for her daughter, who had a congenital heart condition. The little girl had gone through a series of tests and was yet to be scheduled for surgery. Camilla's visa would expire in just over a month and she didn't want to leave her baby behind and go back to Jamaica, especially since the treatment was not available there. Since Shaz met her four weeks ago, she'd turned his life upside down. This latest episode was a case in point.

He strode back to the teenagers, rubbing the hair on his jaw and chin. "Tajon, you're going to mess around and cause an accident."

The young man anchored the metal disc on the leg machine and raised both hands. "Sorry, Shaz. I got distracted for a second." He pointed to the flat-screen television anchored high on the wall facing them.

The teen doing leg presses grinned. "Distracted, my ass."

A sharp look from Shaz and Chris, who was spotting another teen on the bench press machine, had him mumbling. "Sorry."

Chris Deans, a dark-skinned giant of a man and Shaz's good friend, also volunteered at the youth club they started two years ago. They named it the Evanston Gentlemen's Club and used the facilities, adjacent to the community center, to mentor young men in and around Evanston and Chicago.

As he slid the towel from around his neck, Shaz debated whether he had time for a quick shower. "I have to leave, so you're handling the meeting."

"No problem." Chris tipped his close-shaven head to one side. "Trouble on the horizon?"

"That's what I'm trying to prevent."

In the locker room, Shaz grabbed his bag, then shot in and out of the shower in record time. He shrugged into a long-sleeved white shirt and a pair of dress pants he kept handy in his locker. At five in the evening, they were the only concession he'd make to this errand. Though his career as a lawyer demanded a professional look, he avoided being dressed to the gills as much as he could. He secretly hated suits, but preferred them custom-made for a better fit. Now, he rolled back his sleeves, re-tied his locs, picked up his bag, and left the building.

Five more minutes found him downtown, stepping out of an electric blue Alfa Romeo Stelvio SUV and riding the elevator to Darryl Bennett's office. The man served as an alderman and once wielded power at The Castle, a sprawling estate—a city within itself—where Shaz now had a seat on the board of directors. He and Bennett had had several run-ins, all of them to do with Camilla Gibson. Only God knew what he'd find when he made it to the office.

By Miss Mabel's account, Camilla was threatening to do the alderman bodily harm. After what he'd done, she'd be well within her rights to do so. But that wouldn't help her precarious situation.

If nothing else, the woman had chutzpah. Tall and slender, she was no match for Bennett, a strapping man who stood a few inches taller, and had a lot more to lose if things went south between them.

Bennett's office was elegant, with dark wood panelling and heavy sofas more suited to a living room than a waiting area. Shaz stepped around a table laden with magazines and addressed the alderman's receptionist. He'd barely said two words when Camilla's unmistakable accent hit the airwaves around him. "You're a damn liar. If you think I'm going to sit around while you … "

A dozen steps took Shaz to Bennett's office, where he found Camilla stabbing her finger on Bennett's desk, while Miss Mabel clasped both hands to her bosom as if in prayer. When she laid eyes on Shaz, she mouthed, "Thank God, you came."

Standing to one side of Camilla, Shaz gripped her elbow.

She turned wild eyes on him as her nostrils quivered and her lips parted.

With a gentle squeeze to her arm, Shaz murmured, "Now that I'm here, leave this to me, please."

Pointing at Bennett, Camilla spat, "I don't care what arrangement he has with Derrick, he's not getting Ayanna."

Aside from a tic dancing around one of Bennett's eyes, the man didn't move in his seat. He threw a malevolent glare at Camilla before drawing a breath to speak.

Shaz put up a hand to stop him. "Camilla, Miss Mabel, please give me a minute."

After sending the older man a killing look, Camilla swept out with Miss Mabel on her heels. The black ankle-length dress, and her hair pulled into a top knot, highlighted Camilla's regal bearing. At the moment, she might look the part of a queen, but her attitude was far from that of a monarch. If Bennett knew what was good for him, he'd watch himself with this fiery woman.

The second the door closed behind them, Shaz said, "I'm not sure what happened to set this off, but—"

Bennett pointed to the door. "She needs to understand that I've made a *legal* arrangement with the father of the child. I have—"

"I don't care what you have." Shaz fixed his gaze on Bennett. "What I know is, you'd better put a hold on whatever funny business you have going on with Derrick Porter."

Bennett rose from his seat. "You can't come in here and tell me how to run my show."

"And you can't tell me you're so desperate to solve your family problems, you'd take advantage of someone who's here trying to find solutions for her sick baby."

Eyes wide, Bennett gasped. "You're just saying that. As far as I know—"

"You don't know anything, so shut up and listen."

Slowly, Bennett lowered himself to the executive chair.

Shaz folded both arms and held Bennett's gaze. "It doesn't matter that she came to your attention the wrong way, Ayanna Porter is *not* up for adoption. Nor will she be, in this life, or the next. Whatever paperwork or exchange you've done with Porter, consider it null and void."

Moving his head side to side, Bennett smirked. "Life doesn't work like that, Shaz."

"It's Shaz for my friends. Shastra for you. Matter of fact, Mr. Bostwick would be even better."

With both hands splayed on the massive glass-topped desk, Bennett grimaced at the insult. "I don't know what Miss Gibson told you, but my wife and I have a deal with—"

"You clearly didn't hear what I said." Shaz planted his hands on the half-inch-thick glass. "The deal is off."

KNIGHT OF PARADISE ISLAND

Ryan couldn't shake the feeling of being encased in a transparent coffin. The shark cut through the clear, blue water as though coming for him, but it disappeared above their heads. His intuition didn't match the current moment, but he couldn't discount his sense of unease. Every time he ignored his instincts, he landed in trouble.

Aziza threw her head back and grinned over her shoulder, lapping up the experience of tubing through a sealed glass channel inside a giant aquarium filled with some of nature's fiercest aquatic predators. She grabbed his ankles and pointed when the shark's serrated snout entered her line of sight. "Ryan, look."

Her pleasure with everything she experienced delighted him. Ryan loved that about her. Aziza made him view things he took for granted with fresh eyes, which was one of the reasons he was glad he reconnected with her. "I see it, babe."

He wriggled his feet against her side, and she sank her nails in his skin. "Behave."

Laughing, he did the same thing as they slid into an open pool, which signaled the end of the ride. When they left the rubber ring behind, Aziza hugged him as the water cascaded around them. "Thanks for hosting me again. I've loved every minute."

Ryan dropped a kiss on her forehead, then said, "Just returning the favor for showing me your city."

With her hands spread across his back, Aziza scoffed. "You're acting as if you haven't been coming to Evanston since you were a little tiddlywink."

Ryan chuckled. "Whatever that means."

They walked hand in hand onto the sand, and she looked up at him. "Don't forget I knew you when your eyes were where your knees are now."

Ryan threw back his head and laughed. "Says she, who is all of two years younger than I am."

Tugging his hand, Aziza headed for the beach. "Come on, old man."

They sank their feet into the powdery sand, moving toward the one-bedroom bungalow that came with his job at the Paradise Island Grande Resort in the Bahamas. For the last week and a half, they spent most of their nights together in Aziza's room but she had fallen in love with the compact villa that had direct access to the beach via the back-yard. Her appreciation for his home confirmed that while she enjoyed the finer things, she also liked the simple life. The house was nice, but not the height of architectural grandeur.

A half-hour after they showered, Aziza sat between his legs. As he combed out her kinky-curly hair and oiled her scalp, Ryan thought how content he was doing that ordinary task. Fact was, he loved touching her. His mother and father hadn't stayed together, but he remembered scenes like these from his early childhood. At some point, his parents had been in love, but life intervened to separate them. He would not allow that to happen with Aziza.

"You have wonderful hands," she mumbled from the patterned car-pet.

Ryan leaned sideways on the sofa. "So you've told me a time or two, but don't tell me you're about to fall asleep."

"It's your fault." She yawned and pulled herself upright.

"Hmmm. What are we doing for dinner anyway?"

She tipped her head back on the cushion. "Are you for real? After that lunch, I couldn't eat anything more if I tried."

As he chuckled, Aziza ran her fingers along his leg. "I can't believe our time is over already."

He pulled her hair together and secured it with an elastic band. Then he helped her to sit on his lap and stared into her eyes. "Yes, the days went by so quickly."

Aziza trailed a finger across his chin. "You make a great host."

She hesitated over her next words.

After a gentle peck to her lips, he said, "Speak."

"Have you figured out how what we're doing will work?"

A slow smile curved his lips as he thought about the 18-karat gold diamond ring that grabbed his attention in one of the jewelry stores on the property. Aziza deserved that and more. Next time they were together, he'd ask her if she'd put up with him for the rest of her life and slip it on her finger.

"Everything will fall into place when the time is right," he said. "I have a few things I want to tie down, and you need to finish your contract period in Durabia. Next?"

She sighed and brushed his chin with her lips. "You make it sound so easy."

"Babe, it is. As you well know, this isn't a random, feel-good, love-on-vacation deal. We've known each other too long to end up wasting our time." The assessing light in her eyes made him pause. Then he went all in. "Aziza Hampton, I won't rest until we're in the same place working on all our tomorrows."

She cupped his head between her hands and eased his lips open with hers. Their tongues mated in a slow, sensual dance. Aziza held him close as if hungry for him and as though this was the last time they'd be together so she needed as much of him as she could get.

As his body responded, Ryan relaxed against the seat and let her take the lead. She had his shirt halfway up his chest before she whispered, "Let's take this to the bedroom."

After setting Aziza on her feet, Ryan also stood. "I thought we'd never get there."

Later, they would decide where they saw each other in the flesh next. Now, their bodies cried out for the intimate connection they couldn't do without.

Her phone rang, and she sighed against his chest. "I have to get that."

With both hands resting on her hips, he groaned.

Aziza giggled, then kissed his chin. "It'll only take a few minutes. Most likely, it's Mom checking in with me."

She lifted the cellular off the chair arm and swiped the screen, keeping a hand on his wrist. "Hey, Mom. Why are you … "

He gripped her butt and kissed the tiny frown that marked her forehead.

Aziza's gaze cut to his and concern filled her amber-colored eyes that shifted according to her mood. "What happened to Drake?"

Ryan sat and pulled her down next to him. Her expression went from concerned to frightened as she rubbed one side of her face. As if the air had gone out of her, Aziza slumped when the call ended.

"What's up, Zee?" He slid an arm around her shoulder and drew her close.

She sniffled, then met his gaze. "It's Mom. Drake is in the hospital. His wife isn't sure what happened, but they're running some tests."

"D'you want me to get you a flight out tonight?"

She shook her head. "Mom says he's in good spirits, and he's not in too much pain. No sense shelling out money to change my flight when I'm leaving early tomorrow anyway. You've been so generous already."

The joy of having her with him for two weeks meant he hadn't thought twice about flying her to the island. And he'd be willing to spend more for her peace of mind.

"Let's hope you get some rest tonight," he said, smoothing the frown line on her forehead.

"I'll be fine. They'll let me speak with him when they finish the tests." She snuggled into Ryan's side. "As long as we're together, I can deal with anything. Plus, we don't know when we'll be in the same place again."

"As long as you're sure, I want what you want."

She laid her head on his chest. "After we hear from Drake, we'll make some more memories."

Ryan turned her hand over and kissed her palm. "I'll take every moment with you I can get."

The image of that shark coming toward them flashed in his mind, and a weight settled in his stomach. As he caressed the skin on her arm, he sensed that something other than her brother's health issue was on the horizon.

THE SPICE OF LIFE

Anif Montague's breath on her skin pulled Nyoka up short. A mixture of cinnamon and mint, it was cool, fresh, and spicy at the same time. His proximity and the scent he wore left her aroused, distracted, and intrigued.

That hadn't happened since DeWayne. Their relationship classified as a disaster that almost cost her sanity. This past week he had the nerve to contact her via Instagram after she blocked him on every other medium.

Her thoughts settled when she met Anif's piercing gaze. This man could cause her to lose everything.

Still holding a pair of trimming scissors, she cleared her throat and stood straight. Tipping his chin up with one hand, she examined his face at different angles under the light. "You're good to go."

"Thanks." A slight twist of the lips met her smile before he said, "I told you I don't do makeup."

"And I respect that," she replied, with a sharp edge to her voice. "All I did was apply a dab of powder to take the sheen off your skin, and trim your brows a little."

She looked away from his intense eyes, but the air-conditioned dressing room held a bare minimum of furniture—nowhere to escape his scrutiny for long.

When her gaze returned to him, she realized he'd been watching her.

"So you won't consider my offer?"

Shaking her head, she replied, "I've taken a break from modeling."

"Mind telling me the reason?"

She sheathed the scissors as she stepped away from the chair. "I'd rather not. These days, I'm doing makeup exclusively."

What he didn't know was that she'd been modeling since she was seventeen. Along the way, she traveled extensively and earned valuable contracts. With her mother's encouragement, she stayed in school and earned a business degree. Good thing she had. Having her love life entangled with her career caused both to go belly up—a good object lesson in staying focused.

Anif spun the chair and faced the mirror, opening a portfolio on the counter. "What's your number?"

Avoiding his eyes, she studied his locs. "I didn't say I was giving that to you."

"Come on, I'm trying to do business with you."

"Ever heard about taking no for an answer?"

His smile was slow in coming. "If I did, I wouldn't have made it as a writer."

He pulled a card out of the leather case. "Here's my contact information."

She took the linen stock, flipping it between her fingers. The moral clause in her contract prohibited her from connecting with clients outside of the television studio and here she was, flirting with the forbidden.

Thick and neat, the locs tied at his nape made her want to unravel them. Anif towered over her slender frame, and she was tall for a woman. His skin was a creamy caramel and the bottom half of his face was covered in a low stubble that made her fingers itch to touch him. A weird reaction to someone she didn't know.

Then, against what she knew to be a smart move, Nyoka reeled off her cell number.

He smiled and let out his breath, as if he'd been holding it in.

Anif was the first guest today, and she'd been pleasantly surprised when he walked into the dressing room and greeted her in an accent she recognized. Like her, he was Jamaican, and immediately they struck up a conversation.

She discovered he was an indie writer who'd broken out with a best-selling novel. Now, he was back with a follow up book that had surpassed the success of the last one.

When he stood and faced her, she stepped back.

As he smoothed his locs, Anif moved closer and smirked. "Do I make you nervous?"

"Nope, I just don't like people too far in my personal space."

"Understood." The light in his eyes hinted that he saw through her lie. "Don't lose the card. I'd ask you to wait for me after the interview, but I suspect you'd tell me to go jump off someplace really high."

A chuckle escaped from her as she said, "No, my mother raised me right." Then, she winked. "I'd probably be thinking it though."

Anif laughed, a husky sound that captivated her. He was about to respond when the door opened and Libbie, a production assistant, pushed her head inside. "Mr. Montague, we're ready for you on the set."

At the threshold he turned, casual yet suave in a black sweater and jeans. "Don't forget, I'll be calling you."

She didn't respond but stood in front of the mirror placing unused brushes back in their sleeves. Most days, Nyoka arrived at the MLX television station just after dawn to prepare guests for the morning talk show. Her memories tried to crowd her mind but she switched mental gears to Gabrielle, her little angel.

She was now a year old and a beacon of light in Nyoka's life. She'd barely been awake when Nyoka bundled her up and left her with Mrs. Mason—or Aunt Gem as she insisted on being called—their neighbor. The woman was a lifesaver.

"Don't kill yourself hurrying back," had become her goodbye phrase each morning.

Nyoka would laugh and reply, "You're going to spoil us rotten."

Lifting her cosmetic kit, Nyoka hung it over her shoulder, and left the room. She didn't need to walk around the building with the tools of her trade, but one could call it a carryover from her life in Jamaica, plus an overabundance of caution.

Judith, the other makeup artist contracted to the station, had a way of appropriating the items Nyoka left loose, and her tools weren't the only thing the brunette wanted. Nyoka's early slot was a bone of contention, plus her status as the more accomplished and better paid of the two.

As if called by a magnetic force, Nyoka's feet led her down the hall toward the studio. She heard Anif's voice before she saw him. He chuckled with the raven-haired host over something she said, then explained his writing process. Anif was expressive and mesmerizing as he spoke about growing up in Jamaica and incorporating his life in Miami to come up with the plot for his latest novel.

She watched him, fascinated. If she were lucky, he'd forget about calling her. Anif wouldn't be able to handle the dangers and restrictions that came with her complex life. Instinctively, she knew he was a risk she'd be better off not taking.

FIRE IN THE WATER

Unlike the pigeons that happily pecked at crumbs on the dirty sidewalk below her apartment, Brooklyn's own unlucky pigeon, Celeste Francois, felt like a hostage. For several years, she'd been tied and strangled by the ropes of poverty. She'd given in to believing she'd never leave that New York borough and become a dove.

She'd been awake since the sun came on duty earlier, still lying across her full-size bed, summoning all her overweight ancestors to come to her aid.

While the weather outside was warm and welcoming, inside Celeste Francois' tiny apartment, a storm was brewing.

"I am more than a conqueror," she told herself. Unfortunately, no amount of self-convincing or hypnotism in the world could handle all her belly fat. She found ways to camouflage it over the past nine years, off and on, by wearing the latest late-night 'Get-Skinny-Quick' gimmick that never worked. Her daily routine consisted of trying to cram her pounds of all the post-pregnancy fat into a pair of plus size jeans.

"This don't make no doggone sense," she pined, groaning with all the effort. "I just bought these a month ago." She rolled her eyes to the ceiling while thinking of a million other things she'd rather do on her thirty-fifth birthday.

"Mama, please hurry. We're hungry."

The plea came from her ten year-old identical twins, Jeanette and Jonnay, her mini-me opinionated girls. When they weren't working her nerves, she did everything to spoil them. She had very little, but was filled with determination to give the pair of energetic, coffee-colored, four foot ninety pounds of pig-tailed, dawn-to-evening questioning kids, the love and attention she'd never received.

Looking away from Celeste, the twins twisted their lips trying to hide the sneer they knew might bring them closer to a threat of a spanking than they'd want.

Under her steely gaze, they swallowed their comments but glanced at each other. With complaints silently shared—a twin-thing they'd learned at a young age—they continued struggling to balance a huge box between them.

Though the twins had remained silent, tt didn't stop Celeste from ranting as though she'd read their minds. "Will you two just stop aggravating me?" Celeste snapped. Sweat popped from her forehead as she motioned to herself. "You two see I'm trying to get dressed."

Jeannette, a bit older than her twin by almost three minutes, replied dryly, "Ain't nobody trying to aggravate you, Mama. One of them moving men say they done you a favor even coming here yesterday, and today. He said he's gonna just put the rest of your 'crappy' stuff back on the truck." She took a deep breath. "He say he's gonna drive off if you don't pay them the rest of they money."

Jeanette quickly lifted her chin and nodded at her twin. "Didn't he say that, Jonnay?"

Jonnay, following her sister's lead as always, sighed. "He sure did." Jonnay's hands jerked as she shifted her end of the box, filled to the top with her mama's good dishes. "And I'm getting tired."

Celeste moaned, and stared at the ceiling. She grimaced, and then set her face in a determined mask despite the pain.

Maybe it was tiredness that made Jonnay forget her second-place status. She went full rogue and wasn't through complaining.

"That other man," she began, "the one smelling like a skunk wearing bad vanilla—like you always say when somebody is stinking—said that 'cause you went out a time or two wasn't enough reason to let you slide on the rest, Mama." She sped up to get the rest of her report out. "He was even winking like something was in his eyes when he said to tell you that. And then he said, real loud, like he wanted everybody outside to hear, that y'all can discuss it like yawl used to." She hunched her shoulders adding, "Whatever that means."

"Yeah, but—" Jeanette chimed in. "That other man with those black ashy ears like a homeless bunny rabbit said there wasn't gonna be no discussion. Just pay him his—" she frowned. "He said a bad word— money."

Defeated, Celeste dropped her head to her chin. Struggling, Celeste threw her head back onto the pillow. "C'mon now." She gritted her teeth. Her hips bobbed like two overripe cantaloupes with stretch marks. "Finally," she announced as the jeans made its way to her waist without getting anything caught in its zipper.

Celeste slid off the side of the bed and didn't so much as blink. She gestured with a flip of one hand, ordering, "Pick up that box." Then, she slipped into a pair of house shoes that once had two-inch heels. Over time, her weight had turned them into a pair of no-inch flats. "Lay it in the corner next to the refrigerator."

Jonnay scanned the room, then looked at her sister as though waiting for Jeanette's approval to speak. Her brown eyes narrowed as she inquired, "Mama, where's the rest of the kitchen? When we got here last night, I thought it was bigger."

"Yeah , mama," Jeanette, added. "The last three places we lived we didn't have to walk out of it and turn around to get to the stove." She tossed the question to her sister. "Ain't that right, Jonnay?"

Jonnay nodded. "Didn't have to think about opening the fridge first to get inside the oven or the other way round, too."

Celeste frowned at the girls, resting her hands on her massive hips. Her head swung between them, giving each the old Southern Mama's 'evil eye'.

The girls gulped and swallowed whatever words were on the tip of their tongues as they trotted away to do as they were ordered.

Celeste hung her head, whispering a prayer. "Lord, how long do I have to live like this? Can I at least catch a break on my birthday?" Not waiting for an answer, or truly expecting one, she opened the door and waddled down to the steps from her one-bedroom, third-floor walk-up apartment.

"Those girls deserve better than this," she whispered. "It doesn't make no sense I need to keep moving because I don't always have the rent." Winded, she stopped and rested against a wooden bannister for a moment.

Two flights down to go and two angry men: one wanting money, the other want "something" more. Celeste simply wanted some peace of mind and a better life for her girls. And, if life would finally be so kind, she'd also like to get her hands around Sanjay Thomas' neck and send him to meet his maker.

HEAVEN CAN BE HELL

Averic's head snapped upward at the annoying static sound that snatched him from preparing for his sermon.

"Be warned; all verified hell is about to visit you," Aunt Peaches blasted from the intercom.

"Say what?" Startled, the six-foot-five, thirty-five-year-old shot forward in his chair. The sudden movement caused him to scrape his knee against the side of the desk. He grimaced at the sudden bite of pain as he pressed the intercom's button. "Say that again."

Being out of breath and inhaling quickly caused a slight hiccup to escape in her excitement. She blurted in her signature rapid-fire and politically incorrect manner, "Well, nephew-pastor, it's a warm and lovely May afternoon, and I know you studying so you can preach everybody to Paradise come your turn next Sunday morning, especially since you figuring you gonna become senior pastor in a few weeks—"

Averic sighed his frustration. For a while, rumors were going around the church and town that his gossipy widowed aunt was looking for a new husband. Aunt Peaches, built like a rusty-colored beer keg, was seen in some of her pre-saved life hangouts trying to use her old fleshly equipment as unwanted collateral. He didn't want her feelings hurt or someone getting shot, since she was also a licensed concealed gun carrier. Feeling obligated, Averic hired her to be his assistant. And that's when the real fun began.

Today, he had promised to meet with Pastor's Aid Committee heads Mama Mae-Aye and Trustee Black Mack to discuss the upcoming retirement benefit for the current senior pastor. *I might as well pull out the checkbook. They're gonna tell me how cheap I am and that five thousand dollars couldn't buy a decent tablecloth.* He was sure that the Lord himself popped Tylenol every time those two old shysters complained. However, he still didn't appreciate his aunt's reference.

"Let me remind you again," Averic said slowly, still massaging his sore kneecap, "I don't want you comparing any meeting I have with our members to a session in Hell."

The sound of a small, exasperated gasp filtered through the intercom. Aunt Peaches lowered her voice, adding in a more respectful, yet reprimanding tone, "Well please forgive me, Wanna-be-a-Senior Pastor-elect-Reverend-Doctor-Averic Domingo. As your late mama's only sister and your once-favorite auntie, I was just tryin' to tell you that Mama Mae-Aye and Trustee Black Mack can't make their scheduled meeting."

"Seriously?" He could have stayed home and packed for his upcoming trip instead of traipsing across town to the church to get his feelings hurt in what was sure to be a geriatric beat down.

A chuckle quickly replaced the stern measure in Aunt Peaches' voice. "Actually, I overheard a conversation while I was in the second stall in the second-floor ladies' room."

Averic slapped a hand to his forehead harder than he had meant to. *The devil is a liar.* The last thing he wanted was that mental picture to accompany his aunt's confession.

"Ain't no secret that all kinds of truths and such can be learned from any second stall in the ladies' bathroom all over the world," she said, oblivious to the fact that she was making lunch an impossible thing. "Like I said, they're gonna go over to Shout Now Community Church for their Elders' Day celebration this evenin'."

"Thank you for all your *extra* info," Averic replied slowly, knowing from past conversations during Thanksgiving dinners, barbecues, and every other family-related occasion that it would be fruitless to remind her of her fondness for giving too much information. Instead, he replied, "Well, since they canceled and we've discussed not having any *hellish* meetings," he paused, making certain his point still carried, "and I don't have another meeting scheduled this afternoon, I'm leaving so I can get to the airport and make it to the Annual Honolulu Singles and Married Couples retreat in Hawaii for the next few days."

As a further reminder that she should not have tacked something else on his schedule, he added, "I hope to meet with Minister Craig during his Couples Retreat function."

"Hold up, I wouldn't exactly say you don't have any other meetings today," Aunt Peaches told him in a manner that suddenly sounded a bit more serious than necessary.

Averic froze in the middle of returning his documents to a manila folder. "What do you mean?"

"I mean, you can't go home because *now* you *do* have another meeting." Her high-pitched nasal voice returned as she cautioned, "It's someone who hasn't been here in a while. I guess she's overdue for a visit."

Peaches' voice betrayed her as a sudden snicker came over the intercom, masking her mocked concern.

Averic's eyes rolled in pure frustration. "Well, whoever *she* is, I don't have time to meet with her. I'm certainly not in the mood for any confusion right now. Let one of the deacons deal with whatever problem she has."

"Deacon Slipp," Aunt Peaches blurted. "He seen her first and he passed the word onto me. He may be about my age, but he's too old for this new-fangled mess younger folk bringing to the church. He said he knew trouble when he seen it and his power of discernment had told him that he wasn't missing no five-dollar Mighty Wing special at Church's Chunky Chicken to handle it."

The loud sound of Aunt Peaches' wheezing echoed. "So, it looks like you'd better *make* time, and as much as it pains me to say it, you gotta take a hit for the church's sanity team. Besides, you supposed to stay prayed-up." She lowered her voice. "I'd stay and sit in this particular meeting with you, but I ain't that saved yet."

Aunt Peaches' sometimes-zany remarks still managed to catch him off guard, but admitting something like that last part put him on notice. His nose twitched as though he could smell the always pleasant aroma of his Acqua Di Gio cologne fading, his plane ticket to Hawaii for three days disappearing into volcanic smoke, and the acrid smell of Hell's sulfur permeating the office air.

"Okay," he snapped. "Send whoever *she* is in here. It's my charge to keep. Who is it?"

"Glad you finally got around to asking because she's waiting inside the sanctuary. You ain't seen that heffa in a long time. I hoped you'd never see her again."

Choosing to ignore Aunt Peaches' devilish reference to someone being a "heffa," he replied, "Well, bring her inside, please. I really want to get out of here as soon as possible."

"Not as soon as you'll wanna be," Aunt Peaches replied angrily. "because it's your wife. I still can't figure out why her mama named that hellion Heaven."

CHOICES

Seven years ago, Anna was single. Single and happy serving the Lord. Her Harlem, New York-based church was her refuge, and at age nineteen, without any close family for support, the church filled that void.

That year, most of the single women in the congregation were either preparing for marriage or getting pregnant, hopefully after marriage or they got a ring. Anna was one of a handful from the one hundred members who had claimed neither. "I got Jesus, and He's enough," was her anthem. It didn't mean she didn't date on the side. It did mean that she would never testify or let the church know she did, especially the Church Mothers.

And then, as if a bolt of lightning had struck, the Mothers Board realized Anna had avoided the continuous Matrimonial "Sadie

Hawkins" day event. During one of the evening services, a visiting Prophet called for a five-dollar prophetic line. Anna did not have five dollars. If she had, she wouldn't have stood in that particular line anyway.

In her mind, only the visiting Prophet would make a profit, and it was hardly worth her while to subtract from her meager earnings. She was already indebted to paying tithes.

However, on a Thursday night during one of the fifty-two weekly Building Fund Revivals, Nabal Miller stepped through the doors of her church for the first time. He wasn't hard to miss in a congregation where women of all ages, shapes, and financial situations outnumbered the men by ten to one and a half. The half meant a couple of men were still on the "We ain't quite sure about brother so and so, list."

Anna recalled something exotic about Nabal that made the congregation pay attention, especially the Church Mothers. There were whispers that evening. "Who that? He looks so handsome. We ain't seen too many men with pretty gray eyes and that butter complexion."

Heads of dyed-black, and sometimes shades of light blue or purplish hair, covered with white crocheted crowns, popped up like bobble-head dolls in the pews. The women had buns pulled back tight enough to make their faces look ten years' worth of Botox younger.

The feverish offbeat rhythm of the drums chimed in with the rapid clang of tambourines. The clamor covered the spirited and fleshly words of admiration spreading from pew to pew.

"Y'all see that army uniform? My, my, I wish he'd keep my 'Southern country' safe," voiced several of the thirsty 'somewhat saved' women.

No one had a clue that the crisp green uniform with all its medals,

Choices: Standing in the Gap or Standing in God's Way? 11

his high yella, freckled face, and large gray eyes hid the real man. Not even the spiritual "God-done-showed-me-everything" women had seen it.

However, somehow that same night, one of the Church Mothers, according to her, experienced a sudden visit from the spirit realm. "The spirit showed me that this man is gonna marry one of our young sisters," Mother Mayhem propha-lied.

No one was more shocked than Anna when out of the blue, she heard her name called. She was already in a secret pre-engagement relationship with another young man from one of the sister churches. He hadn't proposed yet, but she knew it would happen. On more than one occasion, they went too far with groping and teasing, and came close to fornicating. Perhaps, God had shown that impending embarrassment and sin to the Church Mother.

One of the first things Anna learned when she joined her church was obedience. Obeying the Bible was something to strive for; disobeying the church elders, especially the Church Mothers, was a no-plea deal that led to eternal punishment in Hell.

Two days later, during one of the choir rehearsals, she overheard someone mention they had seen her secret 'friend' suddenly appear in Baltimore, Maryland over that past weekend. "Looks like that brother will be coming up under a new ministry," the person added.

Anna wasn't a genius, but it didn't take one to figure out it was no coincidence that within that same time frame, the Church Mother had convinced her and Nabal, God wanted them to marry.

She thought her and God were tight enough that He would have at least given her a better heads up than the sudden disappearance of the young man she wanted to marry.

Anna would never forget how those Church Mothers went into

overdrive trying to get her hitched. She felt like a bounty was on her head, and they were dead set on getting it. They insisted, "because the Lord said so." She did not have time to buy a gown or even something white or off-white. Getting married in January in New York made it almost impossible to find anything white.

The fear of going to Hell for disobedience was reason enough for her to do as the Church Mother prophesied. Nabal feared he might never return from Vietnam, or would come back a disabled person, so what did he have to lose?

One of the Church Mothers insisted the ceremony be in her tiny one-bedroom apartment. "Begin small so you can appreciate the increase," she claimed.

While they chatted, prayed, testified, and gossiped or "shared" as they called it, the Church Mothers hurried around the small kitchen where they prepared the wedding feast. The menu consisted of crispy fried chicken and dirty rice for the main course, and Communion wafers substituted for the bread. The food was greasy and served on two-ply paper plates. The wedding cake was a two-layer pineapple upside-down with a pair of small candles where a bride and groom usually stood.

Of course, Nabal wore his uniform with an assortment of medals, none of which she bothered to ask how he earned.

Anna wore an ugly blue and brown plaid suit. She wore her long, auburn hair plaited in a thick braid that hung midway down her back. Mute and rigid, her large brown eyes vacant as though she were having an out-of-body experience. A few of the invited church members and several 'who just happened to be in the neighborhood' milled around and waited while she stood, vulnerable before a preacher and a groom she didn't know, both preapproved by the Church Mothers.

Choices: Standing in the Gap or Standing in God's Way? 13

Every detail of what she imagined her wedding to be was absent from this "sham" of a wedding ceremony. She was an angry bride who would become an angrier wife. Each time she watched a wedding, whether in person or on television, she grieved for what she lost.

The grief was compounded because she hadn't listened when she'd last spoken with her estranged father. They'd never seen eye- to-eye over many things. If she wanted to go left, her father insisted to go right.

Nothing had changed. As soon as Anna told her father she had married a serviceman, the negative analysis began.

"What makes you think this man is reliable? Where is his family? Didn't you feel that we would've wanted to meet them before you married? Other than you saying you met him at church, we know nothing. We would've learned something about him, but you married so quickly, we didn't even get an invite. He will not be the same when he returns from war. No one ever is."

***

Less than two months later, Nabal prepared to ship off to Vietnam. Anna wasn't ready to go through her pregnancy alone.

Not one of the Church Mothers offered advice or prayer that made sense. After all, they had done the first part. Their absence of caring showed she would have to figure out the rest on her own.

Anna did not want to be pregnant with a baby and with anger. How could those two feelings coexist? With her emotions in free- fall, she didn't know who to be angrier with. Nabal? Why not him? He could have said "no" to being forced into matrimony. But then, so could she.

One of the Church Mothers, out of habit, quoted a scriptural remix and, for Anna, it was the final straw. "God said," she always prefaced her supposed prophetic gifts with those words, 'Let the wheat and the tares grow together,' you figure it out which one of you is the wheat and the other be the tare. You just make sure you two stay together until the Lord separates and judges you."